UPPER ELEMENTARY
MATH LESSONS

UPPER ELEMENTARY MATH LESSONS
Case Studies of Real Teaching

Anna O. Graeber,
Linda Valli,
and
Kristie Jones Newton

ROWMAN & LITTLEFIELD PUBLISHERS, INC.

Lanham • Boulder • New York • Toronto • Plymouth, UK

Published by Rowman & Littlefield Publishers, Inc.
A wholly owned subsidiary of The Rowman & Littlefield Publishing Group, Inc.
4501 Forbes Boulevard, Suite 200, Lanham, Maryland 20706
http://www.rowmanlittlefield.com

Estover Road, Plymouth PL6 7PY, United Kingdom

British Library Cataloguing in Publication Information Available

Library of Congress Cataloging-in-Publication Data

Graeber, Anna Olga.
  Upper elementary mathematics lessons : case studies of real teaching / Anna O.
Graeber, Linda Valli. Kristie Jones Newton
      p. cm.
  Includes bibliographical references and index.
  ISBN 978-1-4422-1196-4 (pbk. : alk. paper) — ISBN 978-1-4422-1197-1 (electronic
: alk. paper)
  1. Mathematics—Study and teaching (Elementary)—Case studies. I. Valli, Linda,
1947– II. Title.
  QA135.6.G728 2010
  372.7'044—dc22

                                                                    2011004542

Printed in the United States of America

Contents

Part II: Perspectives on Teaching: Commentaries

Preface

Teachers benefit from concrete examples that illustrate good practice. With that in mind, we have crafted nine mathematics cases, with accompanying commentaries, which depict real lessons in real classrooms. These are lessons delivered without rehearsal or extraordinary crafting. Thus while each case highlights at least one particular dimension of good teaching, each case also will likely evoke some dilemmas and inspire ideas for improving that lesson and one's own lessons. Although individual teachers can read and learn from these cases on their own, they will likely be more powerfully used in group settings.

The cases present multiple goals of instruction across mathematical topics (meaning of operations, fractions, ratio, measurement, and data) and exemplify an array of underlying principles of good practice. Almost all learning objectives in the cases match objectives in the newly adopted Common Core State Standards for Mathematics.

A special sidebar feature links each case with one or more of the corresponding standards.

Appreciation is owed to more individuals and organizations than we can name. First, we thank our funder, the Interagency Educational Research Initiative (IERI #0115389), which was a combined effort of the National Science Foundation, the U.S. Department of Education, and the National Institutes of Health. Next, we thank our co-researchers on this project, Patricia Alexander, Robert Croninger, and Jeremy Price, who pushed and improved our thinking at every turn, and all of the graduate assistants and post-docs who contributed to the case collection, coding, and writing, especially Kristie Jones Newton. We also thank Patti Belcher, acquisitions editor at Rowman & Littlefield, for seeing the pedagogical value of these cases and for her helpful, speedy assistance. Last, because pseudonyms are used throughout this volume, special appreciation goes to the "real" teachers behind these cases, who graciously let us into their classrooms so that we could share with you these case studies of real teaching.

Although individual teachers can read and learn from these cases on their own, they are more powerfully used in preservice teacher preparation programs, in-service professional development sessions, and school-based inquiry groups. For teacher educators, course instructors, and staff developers, a *Facilitator's Guide* has been written to accompany the text. Please contact Rowman & Littlefield at textbooks@rowman.com on how to access this guide. Features of the *Facilitator's Guide* include:

- **An expanded research base.** Seminal chapters and research articles only referenced in the Guide that facilitators can use to lead discussion and ground the cases even more firmly in theory, research, and practice.
- **Instructional approaches for each chapter.** Key aspects highlighted with analytic comments to guide discussion.
- **Experienced instructor insight.** Three new commentaries written by Kristie Jones Newton, a math methods instructor, describing her approaches and insights in using the cases.
- **Applications of case studies.** Suggestions on using the cases with preservice and in-service teachers.

Alternative Thematic Frameworks

MATHEMATICS INSTRUCTION PRINCIPLES

LEARNER-CENTERED
PSYCHOLOGICAL PRINCIPLES

Knowledge Principle	Cases 2, 6, 7, 8, 9
Strategic Processing Principle	Cases 1, 5
Developmental Principle	Case 4
Motivational Principle	Case 3
Social Context	Cases 4, 5

TOPIC/SUBJECT CONTENTS

Basic Operations	Cases 1, 2, 5, 8
Frac/Dec/Percents	Cases 2, 8
Measurement	Cases 3, 5, 6
Measure Conversion	Cases 4, 5
Geometry	Case 7
Estimation	Cases 3, 8
Data Interpretation	Cases 8, 9

INSTRUCTIONAL LEVEL CONTEXTS

Supplemental Intervention Class	Case 6
Special Education Class	Cases 1, 4
English as a Second Language (ESL) students	Case 5
Heterogeneous/Grade-Level Groups	Cases 3, 7
Advanced Groups	Cases 2, 8, 9

COMMON CORE STANDARDS

Introduction

Anna O. Graeber and Linda Valli

Every teacher understands that knowing what to do in a concrete situation is not the same as knowing how to do it. Engaging students in worthwhile learning requires more than a knowledge of underlying principles of good teaching. It demands considerable practice as well as concrete images of what that teaching might look like in specific situations. To teach in ways that are different from ways we have been taught (through textbooks, worksheets, recitations), we need alternative images. Changing habits of practice, and expanding our notions of what is possible, requires the ability to imagine something different.

The purpose of this book is to create some of those images: descriptive cases of mathematics lessons that represent an array of sound teaching practices. Cases provide a rich source of material for deeper understandings of the complex, ill-structured practice of teaching. Their narrative structure is well suited to capturing teachers' knowledge in practice. Unlike traditional textbooks, "the verisimilitude of cases helps make related theories useful and relevant, decreases the danger of participants developing inert knowledge, and increases the probability that knowledge will transfer to similar situations in the future" (Levin, 1999, p. 148). Judy Shulman (1992) calls cases "a piece of controllable reality" that are positioned between the prescriptive world of textbooks and the messy world of real classrooms. This makes them a particularly useful pedagogical tool. Reading, reflecting on, and discussing how another teacher approached a particular topic, strategy, or concept opens up new vistas for learning.

The pedagogical cases in this book were written from authentic, unrehearsed lessons taught by regular classroom teachers to diverse groups of real students. As a collection, the cases embody the notion that teaching is multidimensional, that it has different characteristics across and within subject matter (Chambliss and Graeber, 2003; Valli et al., 2004).[1] Although each case highlights a particular dimension of good teaching, several cases have features of good teaching in common. These underlying principles of good teaching are discussed in this introductory chapter and the text commentaries and are outlined in the "Alternative Thematic Frameworks" section. The thematic organization chart also identifies particular topics within the cases, aligns cases with the newly adopted Common Core State Standards (2010), and indicates whether the lesson was primarily geared toward students who were below, at, or above grade level. Six of the nine cases are presented with the thoughtful reflections of an array of commentators: a

---

1 See the companion volume, Chambliss and Valli, *Upper Elementary Reading Lessons: Case Studies of Real Teaching* (Lanham, MD: Rowman & Littlefield, 2011).

classroom teacher, a teacher educator, and those with English for Speakers of Other Languages (ESOL) expertise. In addition, Part II of this casebook, "Perspectives on Teaching," presents more general commentaries that analyze good teaching across cases.

We encourage readers to use the thematic organization to guide their case selections, to depart from the customary way of reading a book (i.e., from first chapter to last) and, instead, to purposefully select cases that are most relevant to their situations. As you read a case, think about how the case can inform and help improve your teaching. Only then should readers turn to the relevant commentaries. Reading the commentaries after your own reflection will provide additional opportunities for growth. Because this casebook will often be used with groups, we have included a *Facilitator's Guide* to assist the instructor, staff developer, or group leader.[2]

HOW THESE CASES WERE SELECTED AND WRITTEN

These nine mathematics cases are drawn from a 4-year study of fourth- and fifth-grade mathematics and reading instruction.[3] We selected these grades and subjects because mathematics and reading are arguably the two most important subjects in the elementary school curriculum, yet

2 Contact Rowman & Littlefield at *textbooks@rowman.com* for information on how to access the guide.

3 The work reported herein was supported by the Interdisciplinary Education Research Initiative (IERI #0115389), a combined effort of the National Science Foundation, the U.S. Department of Education, and the National Institutes of Health. The opinions expressed in this book are our own and do not reflect the positions and policy of the National Science Foundation, the U.S. Department of Education, or the National Institutes of Health.

many fourth- and fifth-graders still struggle with foundational literacy and numeracy skills. Because some groups of children are particularly vulnerable in regards to literacy and numeracy, we selected schools for our examples that were culturally diverse and had relatively high rates of students from poor and low-income families (30 to 90 percent of the school population).

Multiple factors were considered in selecting case study teachers, including student achievement, observation data, and nominations. We began by examining student achievement data for our annual pool of approximately seventy teachers, noting, in particular, teachers whose students achieved higher than predicted scores on standardized tests given by the state and school district. We then analyzed data from classroom observers, ranked teachers on their overall high-quality ratings, and made a list of teachers to consider. Members of the research team also asked for written recommendations from observers and met to discuss teachers who were high on one or more criteria (student achievement, observer rating, observer nomination). By the end of that meeting, the team had selected the final group of case study teachers. In addition to selecting teachers who exhibited various characteristics of good teaching in the lessons we observed, we wanted to include a range of contexts: both fourth- and fifth-grade classrooms, classes ranging from special education to gifted and talented, classrooms with a high percentage of English language learners, lessons that focused on different topics and genres, and so forth.

Observers from the team audiotaped and took narrative field notes of each lesson. They interviewed the teachers after each observation, asking teachers to reflect on the lesson, their students, the curriculum, and the school climate. The research team also collected classroom materials, worksheets, and handouts from the case study lessons. Subsequently, members of the team transcribed the tapes and inserted the field notes into the transcripts for analysis. Our mathematics experts, Anna Graeber and Kristie Jones Newton, made the final decision on which lessons were case worthy. A writing team then met regularly to develop procedures for coding cases, to establish a standard protocol for case writing, and to decide on the dimensions of quality to be exemplified in each case.

Because we believe that teaching should be closely guided by understandings of how people learn (Bransford, Brown, and Cocking, 1999), we drew on five research domains that were core to the development of the American Psychological Association's (APA) *Learner-Centered Psychological Principles* (1995). Those domains, used for case selection and development, indicate, for example, that good teachers promote deep, principled learning of content; encourage the development of cognitive and metacognitive skills; motivate students to engage deeply in subject matter; address individual and developmental differences among students; and create inclusive, affirming, and successful learning environments (Alexander and Murphy, 1998). These principles are explicitly brought out in the cases.

But school subject areas, curricular topics, students, and instructional materials make different demands on teachers' content and pedagogical expertise, signaling the importance of drawing on domain-specific research. Although this research is consistent with learner-centered psychological principles, the particular manifestations of exemplary teaching differ by subject matter. This collection of mathematics cases exemplifies instances of good teaching, those occasions in which the teacher presents and maintains high-level tasks while scaffolding as needed, questions students about their thinking, has students explore and discuss alternative methods to solving problems, helps students connect mathematical ideas, and shows the usefulness of mathematics outside the classroom (Kilpatrick et al., 2003; NCTM, 2000).

As mentioned earlier, case commentators were selected who could provide insights on good teaching from different perspectives: special education, second-language acquisition, moral dimensions, cognitive psychology, and subject matter expertise. Wanting both research and practitioner perspectives, we also invited an award-winning principal and an expert elementary school teacher to comment on the lessons. These commentaries bring out the underlying principles and multiple aspects of good teaching. We urge readers to read and reflect on the cases before turning to the commentaries. This will foster both independent thinking and deeper reflection.

WHAT TYPE OF CASES?

The case literature can be divided into two basic categories or ends of a spectrum: dilemma cases and exemplary cases (Barnett-Clarke, 2001). Dilemma cases are structured around problems of practice, such as cross-cultural communications or subject-matter misunderstandings, which require readers to ponder what they would do in that situ-

ation (Carter, 1999; Merseth, 1996; L. Shulman, 1992).
Exemplary cases, on the other hand, are designed to illustrate particular aspects of practice—to depict a teaching
method, classroom organization, or way of interacting
with students. Through their concrete detail, they can illustrate principles of good teaching and ground theoretical
understandings (Merseth, 1996; Shulman, 2004). In this
type of case, "teaching skills or instructional approaches
(e.g., cooperative learning or inquiry teaching) are made
concrete by portraying a teacher using the method in an
actual classroom" (Carter, 1999, p. 167). While both types
of cases can serve multiple purposes (e.g., illustrate theory,
promote reflection, develop problem-solving skills), each is
better suited to accomplish some goals more than others.

We have elected to prepare a book of cases that primarily illustrate, or "exemplify," particular aspects of teaching, but also evoke teaching dilemmas. The cases are not
"exemplary" in all aspects. Indeed, in our observations of
hundreds of lessons we rarely, if ever, saw a lesson that we
would deem "perfect." But we often saw lessons in which
some aspect of sound teaching was highly visible. It is
these features of good teaching that the cases highlight. In
this sense the cases reflect aspects of exemplary cases. And,
knowing how difficult good teaching can be, we wanted
to present some "images of the possible." As Lee Shulman
(1992) writes: "Case studies of . . . well-grounded exemplars of good practice . . . portray concrete human images
of activities and values worthy of emulation. They thus
serve to stimulate . . . alternative forms of practice that are
rooted in real teaching" (pp. 8–9). This does not mean that
every teacher action in every case is perfect. It does mean

that the teaching in these cases is more accomplished, and more difficult, than immediately meets the eye.

But helping teachers consider what might be improved in a lesson is probably even more valuable than providing exemplars. Barnett-Clark (2001) cautions that pure exemplars can oversimplify teaching and call attention to mere surface characteristics, whereas dilemma-focused cases can "pull participants into an inquiry mode" (p. 311). The *Facilitator's Guide* includes questions that will help stimulate readers to consider how a lesson might be improved, whether the teacher might have considered a different approach, or why the approach was "good" for the situation described. Thus, there are dilemmas that arise from the cases. Believing that "a good teacher is not one who can master the teaching model but rather can master diverse situations, that is, come to terms with a wide range of events and contingencies" (Carter, 1999, p. 175), we ask teachers to consider the cases in light of what is known about the context and to ponder some "what ifs" for the cases. If, as Borasi (1994) has suggested, a student's errors in mathematics can serve as "springboards for learning," then the solid but imperfect lessons of a teacher also ought to spark ideas for improvement of that and one's own lessons.

WHY THESE SUBJECT-MATTER CASES?

We have also elected to focus these cases on the teaching of subject matter. Over the past decade or so, education researchers have become increasingly aware of the importance of teachers' knowledge of subject matter for student learning. This has been accompanied by greater understanding of the differences in pedagogical expertise across subject areas and the complexity of learning to teach different subjects (Grossman et al., 2005; Stevens et al., 2005). Because cases enhance teachers' professional knowledge (Lundeberg and Scheurman, 1997) and improve their ability to make well-reasoned decisions (Grossman, 2005), using cases about the teaching of specific subject matter should be a high priority with both preservice and in-service teachers (Shulman, 2004). Wilson's (1992) claim that the subject-matter knowledge needed for good teaching requires new methods still holds.

Recent documents and articles suggest various attributes of "good" or "effective" mathematics instruction. What that usually means is instruction that helps students develop meaningful and lasting understandings, skills, attitudes, and beliefs that will facilitate accurate application of mathematics in a variety of in- and out-of-school contexts. This is a goal that would include but goes beyond that of "score at least at the proficient level" on the state's test for No Child Left Behind standards. It is our desire that the following cases, taken from unrehearsed lessons taught by some brave, but otherwise "regular" elementary teachers, will serve to inspire and inform those teachers seeking ways to incorporate the attributes of good mathematics instruction into their own classrooms.

In addition, since these cases were written, most states across the country have adopted the Common Core Standards for Mathematics. Developed under the leadership of the Council of Chief State School Officers (CCSSO) and the National Governors Association (NGA), these standards are the first widely adopted national attempt to specify the mathematical knowledge and numeracy skills that students would need to be college and career ready. Each of the cases in this volume addresses one of these standards, which are clearly identified in the "Alternative Thematic Frameworks" and on the first page of each case.

PREVIEW OF CASES

There are many different lenses or ways of sorting through the mathematics lesson cases presented in this book. Indeed when we first began looking at the cases, we tended to look for evidence of Alexander and Murphy's (1998) five learner-centered principles. We also considered some specific mathematics education traits such as allowing students to explain their reasoning, discussing alternative methods, and making connections to mathematics applications in the everyday world. One element in each of the titles of the mathematics cases suggests how we viewed the chief strength of each case. However, the titles selected and the discussion provided are but examples of the ways in which the cases can be analyzed. There are many more examples that could be used to highlight the strengths of the lessons or suggest ways of improving the lessons. In the examples below, we highlight a few of the positive examples of the principles being considered. Teachers and facilitators will find others and will also find that examples used to illustrate one principle can simultaneously illustrate another.

Two sets of principles or lenses for viewing the cases are Alexander and Murphy (1998) five learner-centered principles and the principles enumerated in the National Research Council's (2005) publication, *How Students Learn: Mathematics in the Classroom.* Only a few examples drawn from the cases are given as illustrations. Careful study of the cases will reveal many more. While Alexander and Murphy outline principles of learner-centered teaching, the NRC publication approaches teaching and learning from principles of learning. These sets of principles are congruent and, indeed, often draw on the same research bases. Teachers and facilitators will find many connections among them, and some examples of these connections are included below.

LEARNER-CENTERED PSYCHOLOGICAL PRINCIPLES

Principled knowledge refers to concepts and processes that are central to a field of study and that are well connected to other domain-specific concepts and processes. A learning-centered teacher fosters students' principled knowledge. In Case 2, Ms. Smith helps her student, Jacob, not by telling him that his answer of the denominator divided by the numerator (or $4 \div 1$) is wrong, but helping him realize that this leads to a contradiction. Such checking of consequences is a crucial aspect of comprehending mathematics as a logical and connected field. This is consistent with her repeated requests for student justification for specific operations and her questioning to extend the measurement meaning of division by whole numbers to division by fractions.

Ms. Shepard (Case 6) takes the time to help students understand area as not simply a formula (e.g., $l \times w$), but to understand it as the number of square tiles that will fit inside the outline. The notion of area as amount of space or fill inside a boundary is a general concept of area, not one of many formulas ($l \times w$, ½ [hb], ½ h [b_1 + b_2], πr^2). Ms. Shepard makes a similar effort to help students understand the concept of perimeter and why the procedure of the number of edges of square tiles on the border (or adding the lengths of the sides) yields the perimeter.

The *strategic processing principle* involves teachers' modeling, or making public, their reasoning or problem solving. In Case 5, Mr. Forrest attempts not only to have students use measurement conversion to make comparisons, but also to make them aware of strategies useful in problem solving—both in mathematics and in their lives outside of school. He evokes problem-solving strategies from the students, posts them on the board, and toward the end of the case asks students what strategies they used. Ms. Keller, in Case 1, makes explicit why 8×4 will be the number of apples needed for eight pounds of apples. She makes clear how the drawing, showing two sets of four apples, could be extended to 8 such sets and its relationship to 8×4.

Another aspect of strategic processing is helping students become reflective and evaluate their own work (i.e., the teacher is not the sole arbitrator of right and wrong). In the previous discussion of principled knowledge, Ms. Smith's work with Jacob is an example of her helping him find ways to assess his own work. This pedagogical move can be described as both an example of principled knowledge and of strategic processing, an illustration of the fact that the principles are often intertwined.

The *development principle* is evidenced when teachers craft lessons that are matched to the students' cognitive, sociocultural, affective/emotional, and physical level of development. Such teachers maintain high but reasonable expectations for students. Without deep knowledge of students, this is often difficult to observe. However, some lessons and teacher comments allow one to "see" some of these attempts. In the complete transcript of Case 1, for example, Ms. Keller concluded the lesson by telling students that if they have difficulty reading the problems assigned for homework, she will be available during lunch and recess time to help them. When she begins the Case 5 portion of the lesson by reading the question aloud, she likely evidences her understanding that not all of these fifth-grade special education students may be able to read the problems. Nevertheless, this reading difficulty is not considered a reason for avoiding "word problems." When Jervon responds to the milkshake question with answers related to a previous problem, she simply draws him back to the milkshake problem. This teacher move likely reflects Ms. Keller's cognizance of Jervon's problem with focus. Similarly, recognizing that students would be comfortable and perhaps aided in solving the problem by drawing 23 milkshake containers but wishing first to move the class forward in analyzing the information given in the problem, she delays students' drawing until after she has modeled problem analysis.

Teachers enact the *motivation principle* when they reference students' interests, make evident their own enthusiasm for the subject, actively involve students in the lesson, or promote students' positive belief in self-efficacy. Ms. Hinton (Case 3) wishes to have students become more

familiar with metric units and to help them begin to distin-
guish between mass and weight. She involves students with
hands-on experiences involving canned foods (with metric
units indicated). Students compare sizes and grams to gain
some understanding of the concept of a gram. This is not a
rote "about 30 grams equals one ounce" lesson, but rather
a lesson that provides an opportunity for students to see
and lift objects of various gram measures and experience
their associated "heaviness."

The *social context* principle requires not only that the
classroom climate is pleasant, inviting, and respectful of all
students, but that students have at hand the needed resources and guidance. The principle also concerns the social
interaction patterns; the interaction patterns established for a
lesson should be supportive of the goal of the lesson, and the
teacher should welcome and engage students' contributions.
In Case 5, Mr. Forrest elicits and posts students' notions
about strategies. He also accepts the strategies students offer
and honors their thinking behind a card pairing of measurements (type of unit), which was not his original intent. His
organization of whole class discussion about strategies and
skills, the small group card ordering-pairing activity, and
group presentation to the whole class seem consistent with
his lesson goals. He himself interacts with and encourages
the groups without solving the tasks for them.

NATIONAL RESEARCH COUNCIL'S
PRINCIPLES OF LEARNING

An alternative framework around which to introduce the
cases is that of the National Research Council's (NRC's)

2005 publication *How Students Learn: Mathematics in the Classroom*. The authors outline three principles of learning that "are important for teachers to understand and be able to incorporate in their teaching" (p. 1). These principles are based on work in the cognitive sciences and are highly compatible with suggestions found in the National Council of Teachers of Mathematics publications such as the 2000 *Principles and Standards for School Mathematics* and the 2003 *Research Companion to the Principles and Standards for School Mathematics*. The principles are:

1. Students come to the classroom with preconceptions about how the world works, if their initial understanding is not engaged, they may fail to grasp the new concepts and information, or they may learn them for purposes of a test but revert to their preconceptions outside the classroom.
2. To develop competence in an area of inquiry, students must (a) have a deep foundation of factual knowledge, (b) understand facts and ideas in the context of a conceptual framework, and (c) organize knowledge in ways that facilitate retrieval and application.
3. A "metacognitive" approach to instruction can help students learn to take control of their own learning by defining learning goals and monitoring their progress in achieving them. (NRC, 2005, pp. 1–2)

Taking students' preconceptions into account is one consideration of teachers who honor the first of these principles. A number of the case lessons have examples of teachers

taking into account or building upon students' initial understanding. Mr. DiLoretto (Case 7) appears to understand that
his students' everyday understanding of "volume" may not
help them explore the volume of solid objects. On the other
hand, he strives to build on everyday usage when that makes
sense. For example, he asks students to determine attributes
of their parents before discussing the more abstract idea of
attributes of geometric shapes.

Ms. Hinton (Case 3) knows that many students are
compelled to believe the notion that if two objects are the
same size, they are the same weight (one instance of Stavy
and Tirosh's [2000] intuitive rule, same A ⇒ same B). Ms.
Hinton in fact evokes this commonly held notion as a way of
launching her lesson on aspects of the metric system.

In scaffolding a student who is struggling to determine
how one might find how much of an ingredient is needed
for one-half a recipe, Ms. Smith (Case 2) presents a similar
problem: What do you do to double a recipe? This is an
attempt to link "one-half" to a process of doubling, which
most students would find quite intuitive. Similarly, when
Mr. Wilson's advanced students (Case 9) have difficulty
seeing the difference between a graph of discrete data and
graphs of continuous data, Mr. Wilson scaffolds for them.
Rather than telling them what the difference is or providing a definition, he explicitly points to the unbroken line
in a number of continuous data graphs and asks them for
the difference in the discrete data graph (composed of
unconnected dots).

Developing competence in mathematics includes fostering understanding of concepts and making conceptual connections. Concepts that are needed to build the conceptual

frameworks, discussed in principle 2 above, are given meaning by using multiple representations. Ms. Shepard's Case 6 lesson on perimeter provided at least three different representations of the perimeter of a rectangle (a physical trace, the line segments on a diagram, and the formula for the perimeter). This use of multiple representations likely helps students form images and foster connections between the notion of "perimeter" and the symbolic representation. This helps ground what some might consider a "fact" (namely the perimeter of a rectangle is $2L + 2W$) with the concept of perimeter.

Another example of grounding facts within conceptual understanding is Ms. Hinton's (Case 3) use of "real world" objects to help students gain a sense of the "gram." Cited in the previous discussion of learner-centered teaching as an example of the motivational principle (active participation), here one can view that use of experience with the grocery items as a means of building conceptual understanding—not merely a rote idea. Note that the scenario indicates Ms. Hinton's lesson opened with a review of metric prefixes (factual knowledge) that included connections about their meanings (e.g., "cent" and hundredths as a cent is part of one dollar). Although the meanings of the prefixes can be regarded as knowledge of conventions or mere "facts," Ms. Hinton makes efforts to foster her students' ability to connect these conventions with other knowledge they likely have.

Ms. Fulton (Case 8) makes use of a newspaper report about students being "bullied" to help her students realize the impact of sample size. This example, together with their jellybean sampling experiences, helped students build a conceptual understanding of the relationship between sample size and accuracy of prediction to the population. This lesson may not only help students understand the importance of sample size but also help them define, generalize, or extend the meanings of "samples." It is not just food that is "sampled" (a process with a conflicting real-world meaning), but also groups of people.

Metacognitive approaches involve helping students monitor their own progress and assess their work. In the opening whole-class activity (board work presented by students) of Case 2, Ms. Smith repeatedly asks the student presenter to give reasons for the steps taken in problem solving: How do you know 25 percent is 1/4? Why did you subtract? Why did you add the 5 percent? This not only makes the students' reasoning public for the benefit of the entire class, but it serves as a model for students to internalize as they do mathematics. Is adding the correct operation? Is the substitution I made really an equivalent form?

Ms. Keller in Case 4 models questions to ask when confronted with a problem: Do I understand what the problem is asking? What information is given? What am I looking for? When a student responds to the second question with a solution for solving the problem, Ms. Keller accepts the strategy as plausible but adds the given information and then presses on for more of the given information. Used with consistency and explicit directions for the students to ask such questions of one another and themselves, these strategic processes can lead to students' adoption of the process. (Elementary teachers may recognize this as a mathematics class equivalent of Palinscar and Brown's [1984] "reciprocal teaching" work in reading.)

As the authors of *How Students Learn* point out, "support for self-assessment is provided by opportunities for discussion where teachers and students can express different views and explore which ones seem to make the most sense" (NRC, 2005, p. 12). Examples of such community critique of ideas can be seen in Ms. Hinton, Case 3, both within the small groups and in the whole class setting. Ms. Hinton asks students to offer ideas on reasonableness and what generalizations are suggested by the examples they have used.

The examples given above are not presented to limit discussion or to suggest that the comments present a unique way of viewing the lesson events. Rather they are to suggest that these not-perfect lessons include numerous examples of quality teaching. Nor do we mean to suggest that the learner-centered and NRC principles are the only lenses through which the lessons may be viewed. There are others. For example, teachers may wish to look for instances of the six principles for school mathematics or the five process standards as defined in NCTM's *Principles and Standards for School Mathematics* (2000) or the "Standards for Mathematical Practice" described in the introduction to the Common Core State Standards for Mathematics. It is our desire that the examples presented here will help others find meaningful ways of viewing, critiquing, and learning from these cases.

CASE STRUCTURE AND ORDER

The eight teachers portrayed in these cases range in experience from one to over forty years. All but one are

European American; Ms. Fulton is African American. All eight of the teachers had culturally diverse classrooms of students, which we describe in the case overviews by using the school district's official categories: African American, Asian, Hispanic, and white. Although somewhat limiting and awkward,[4] these categories provide us with the most comprehensive and systematic data available.

We also use three acronyms, taken from official records, to describe the student population: FARMs, ESOL, and IEP:

- FARMs stands for Free and Reduced Meals and is an indicator of poverty.
- ESOL stands for English for Speakers of Other Languages and is used to identify English language learners who were assigned to these supplementary classes based on their levels of English language proficiency.
- IEP stands for Individualized Education Plan and denotes special education students.

Because students sometimes move in and out of these categories, and because their school history is relevant, we use the school district phrase "were currently or had been" in our case overviews.

To prepare the reader for the case narrative, we begin each case by describing the setting and giving a general

---

4 For example, some students classified as African American had been born and raised in countries of Africa, whereas many students classified as Asian had been born and raised in the United States. We have no information regarding the classification of the growing numbers of Arab Americans and recent immigrants from the Middle East.

overview. Where relevant, we also ask the reader to work out the mathematical problems the students have been given (included in the *Facilitator's Guide*). Knowing something about the teacher, students, time of year, classroom, and case content gives a sense of "being there" and helps us better understand teachers' actions.

The order of the math cases was determined by the mathematics content, following the order in which the mathematical content strands are presented in the NCTM's (2000) *Principles and Standards for School Mathematics*. For the content strands represented in the cases the order is: Number and Operations (Cases 1–2), Measurement (Cases 3–7), and then Data Analysis (Cases 8–9). Within these strands, the cases are presented, roughly, in the order of difficulty of the topic.

We encourage readers to picture themselves in the classroom, watching the lessons unfold, or even participating in the activities. As you read, think about the teachers' pedagogical moves, what they were trying to accomplish, and what you might have done in that situation. Raise questions and reflect on the questions at the end of the case. Use the titles, which highlight important aspects of teaching, this introduction, and the "Alternative Thematic Frameworks," presented earlier, to guide your selections. Remember that these are not raw transcripts of lessons you are reading, but cases carefully crafted to serve as tools for teaching and learning about teaching.

I
THE TEACHING
OF MATHEMATICS:
LESSON CASES

Case 1
Promoting One of the Meanings of Multiplication: Requesting Alternate Methods in Order to Foster Understanding

Fifth-Grade Mathematics Lesson

CASE SETTING

This case is part of a longer lesson on converting units of measurement (Case 4), but the special education students needed review/reinforcement of this basic meaning of multiplication that is addressed in a Grade 3 Common Core Standard. Taught by Evelyn Keller, a special education teacher at Brookfield Elementary, the class lasted one hour. All seven students had IEPs; three were African American and four were Hispanic who were also attending ESOL classes. About two-thirds qualified for FARMs. Ms. Keller was the students' only mathematics teacher. She had been teaching for thirty-four years and had her own small room, close to the front office. Students sat at long tables facing the front board. In this case, we focus on the parts of the lesson where Ms. Keller requests alternative methods from her students.

CASE OVERVIEW

The following excerpt is from a class where the teacher attempted to help students understand when multiplication is an appropriate method of solving problems and how it is related to repeated addition. Rather than telling the students to multiply, she asked the students for a "shortcut" after drawing the same picture repeatedly. The intent of the scenario is to illustrate how this teacher used the request of an alternate method as a way to promote an understanding of multiplication.

Before assigning this case, ask your students to answer this math question in preparation:

"Rochelle bought eight pounds of apples for pies. If each apple weighs four ounces, how many apples did she buy?" Explain how you got your answer.

RELATED COMMON CORE STATE STANDARD

Grade 3
Operations and Algebraic Thinking
Standard 1:

- Interpret products of whole numbers, e.g., interpret 5×7 as the total number of objects in 5 groups of 7 objects each. *For example, describe a context in which a total number of objects can be expressed as 5×7.*

THE CASE

Ms. Keller asked Danny to draw a picture to represent four gallons. "Four gallons is how many cups?" she asked. Ms. Keller specified that she wanted Danny to draw the number of cups in one gallon. Danny figured out that there were sixteen cups in a gallon. "Okay. Now, can you figure out how many cups there are in four gallons?" she asked. "You could keep drawing them all and counting them but can you think of a shortcut?" Danny responded that he could just multiply sixteen times four. Ms. Keller praised his work and moved on to work with another student.

Later during the class, Ms. Keller posed a problem from the book. She read, "Rochelle bought eight pounds of apples for pies. If each apple weighs four ounces, how many apples did she buy?" After discussing the relevant information in the story, Ms. Keller asked for a suggestion for tackling the problem.

One student suggested that they "put the rule down." Ms. Keller responded that "sixteen ounces equals one pound." A student then suggested counting by fours so the answer would be in ounces. "Okay," said Ms. Keller. "You're going four, plus four, plus four." The student took over at this point. "Now plus four one more time," he said.

"So how many apples is that?" asked Ms. Keller. "Four," said the student. "Okay," said Ms. Keller, "that's four apples." She drew apples on the board as she said, "There's an apple, there's an apple, there's an apple, there's an apple. So if I get four apples together that equals sixteen ounces and that's the same as . . .?" A student responded that sixteen ounces was a pound, and Ms. Keller added that four apples also equals one pound.

A student then insisted that Ms. Keller draw another four apples to get two pounds, and she responded by drawing four more apples. "Keep doing it until you get eight pounds," he said. Ms. Keller said they could do that but suggested there was not enough room on the board. "Anyone got a shortcut . . .?" she asked.

"You could go eight times four," suggested a student. Ms. Keller elaborated on the student's suggestion. "Because I'm going to do this eight times. I've got four in each row. And eight times four equals . . . ?" Several students gave thirty-two as the product. "Thirty-two what?" asked Ms. Keller. "Apples," said several of the students.

QUESTIONS

1. Why did Ms. Keller refer to multiplication as a "short-cut"?
2. Why did Ms. Keller push for a "short-cut"? Was it appropriate to do so?
3. What should Ms. Keller do if the students use repeated addition again in the next problem?
4. What other "short-cuts" can you think of that are appropriate for fifth-graders?

Case 2
Fractions, Decimals, and Percentages: Evoking Student Reasoning

Fifth-Grade Mathematics Lesson

CASE SETTING

Brittany Smith, a third-year teacher at Hawthorne Elementary School, taught this lesson one late spring afternoon. In her large classroom, one of several portables in the back of the main school building, students sat in groups at round tables. This was an advanced class, where the sixteen students were expected to work on a sixth-grade level. A third of these students had been or were currently in ESOL classes and 25 percent were or had been in the FARMs program. Half the students were of Asian heritage, 42 percent white, and 8 percent Hispanic. This particular lesson was a review of fractions, decimals, and percentages.

CASE OVERVIEW

The following excerpt is from a mathematics class where students were routinely asked to give reasons and the teacher attempted to help students apply prior knowledge to a puzzling situation. The scenario illustrates ways in which the teacher attempts to help students make public links between their use of procedures or operations and the reasons for doing so. This would seemingly help not only the answering student but also those listening (Hiebert, 2003). It may also establish the expectation that reasons exist and are required in this classroom. Ms. Smith's interactions with individual students also illustrate ways in which she prompts them to bring prior knowledge to bear on new problems. This again may prompt students to develop a habit of mind in which they learn to bring their own prior knowledge to new situations rather than feeling helpless in mathematics and relying on others for answers or merely putting puzzling problems aside (NRC, 2001).

RELATED COMMON CORE STATE STANDARD

Grade 6
Ratios and Proportional Reasoning
Standard 3c:

- Find a percentage of a quantity as a rate per 100 (e.g., 30% of a quantity means 30/100 times the quantity); solve problems involving finding the whole, given a part and the percentage.

THE CASE

Ms. Smith began the class with a problem about beach towels on sale. She asked the students what the sale price would be for a towel that regularly costs $12 but was on sale for 25 percent off. For students who finished early, she asked them to find the total price by adding 5 percent sales tax.

After the students completed the problem, Ms. Smith requested volunteers to share the solution. A girl named Madura went to the board and wrote: $12/1 \times 1/4 = 12/4 = 3/1$. "How do you know that you can use one-fourth for 25 percent?" asked Ms. Smith. Madura said she converted it into a fraction, but she did not explain how she knew it was one-fourth. The teacher responded, "You converted it into a fraction. And how did you do that?" The girl stated that she had turned the percentage into a decimal and then recognized the decimal as being equivalent to a benchmark fraction—a common one that she had memorized. Ms. Smith reminded the girl that they had learned how to change one-fourth to a decimal, but now it was "one of them that we just know." A student reiterated, "It's stuck in our minds."

As Madura continued with the solution, Ms. Smith stopped her again to ask why she subtracted $3 from $12 (rather than adding it). The student responded by stating it was a discount. Ms. Smith added that a discount is something you take away from the regular price. The board work concluded with Madura stating that the sale price was $9 and Ms. Smith praising her work.

Ms. Smith then requested a volunteer to figure out the sales tax. Jacob volunteered, and Ms. Smith asked that he tell the class what he is doing as he writes. He explained that he was finding 5 percent. The teacher clarified for the class by stating, "Okay, so you're taking $9 and multiplying it by 5 percent. And I can see that you took 5 percent and you changed it into what form?" Jacob said that he turned it into a decimal. The teacher elaborated by saying that Jacob "found the equivalent decimal."

After determining the sales tax, Jacob stated that the total price was $9.45. Ms. Smith then asked the class why "Jacob took his 5 percent and he added it instead of subtracted it?" A student responded that percentage off would be subtracted but tax is added on. Again, Ms. Smith elaborated by saying, "Okay. There's a difference between a discount and tax. Tax is something that we add on at the end, right? That's the money that the state gets from us."

Ms. Smith turned the students' attention to the test review on their tables. After a brief discussion, the students began working independently. As the students worked, Ms. Smith began to move from small group to small group providing feedback.

Later during the class, Ms. Smith noticed Jacob struggling and sat down at his table. "How do you take a fraction and turn it into a decimal?" asked Ms. Smith. "Divide the denominator by the numerator?" speculated Jacob. Rather than telling Jacob that he was incorrect, Ms. Smith asked again, "What do you have to divide?" Jacob repeated himself, stating that you divide the denominator by the numerator. Ms. Smith changed her question slightly, but Jacob gave her the same response for a third time.

Ms. Smith proceeded to use a familiar benchmark fraction to help Jacob see a contradiction. "Okay. If I give you this fraction, one-fourth, how do you write that as a decimal?" Jacob said, "Twenty-five hundredths." Ms. Smith then asked what four divided by one would be, but Jacob said "twenty-five." She asked again, but Jacob gave the same answer. Persisting, Ms. Smith asked, "Jacob, what's four divided by one? What's any number divided by one?" Finally, Jacob appeared to see the contradiction. Ms. Smith finished by asking, "So what number are we dividing? We have to take the . . ." Together, they established that it is the numerator that must be divided by the denominator, not the other way around. Ms. Smith then returned to the original problem and helped Jacob apply the same idea.

The students continued to work and Ms. Smith praised and assisted them. After a while, a student asked her about finding the amount of ingredients for half a batch of something. Ms. Smith started by asking the student about something more familiar. "Okay. For half a batch. All right, so when you wanted to double a batch, what did you do to each ingredient?" This seemed to be no problem for the student. "You add two more to it. Actually, you multiply it." Ms. Smith pushed for more detail. "And what did you multiply one and one-fourth cups times?" The student responded with a "two."

Ms. Smith returned to the half-batch problem. "Times two. Okay, because you wanted to double that, so you multiply times two. Now, if you want . . . a half batch, what are you going to multiply by? You're going to take one and one-fourth and multiply it by . . . ?" The student responded with another "two." Ms. Smith reminded the student that multiplying by two would produce a double batch. She asked again. "What do you multiply by if you want a half a batch?" The student replied with "one-half."

Ms. Smith proceeded to other tables, checking students' progress and assisting students who needed it. While helping a student with a division problem involving fractions, Ms. Smith appealed to their understanding of division in general. "Okay, you've got three and a half teaspoons of salt, right? Okay, for every batch of flour, or of brownies, that you make you need half a teaspoon of salt—half a teaspoon, half a teaspoon, half a teaspoon. We're going to take our three and a half teaspoons and we're going to divide it into piles that are each one-half teaspoon. How many piles are you going to end up with?"

When the student questioned her, Ms. Smith responded by using an example with whole numbers. "Okay, now, think about it like this. If I had twelve eggs, okay, and I said I'm going to make groups of three—group of three, group of three, group of three. How many groups would I end up with?" The student responded with "six." Ms. Smith decided to draw a picture of twelve eggs. She circled groups of three until she had included all eggs in a group. "Okay. So I have one group, two groups, three groups, four groups, right? So I took twelve eggs, I divided them into groups of three, right? So twelve divided by three is four. So there are four groups, right?"

Having established the answer to the division problem with whole numbers, Ms. Smith returned to the original problem. "You've got three and a half teaspoons of salt, okay. Now, you've got to take those three and a half teaspoons and divide them into piles that are one-half teaspoon, right? So three and a half divided into . . . ." The student interrupted by answering, "seven batches of brownies." Ms. Smith praised the student's work and moved along and checked the progress of other students.

The students continued to work and Ms. Smith continued assisting them. Ms. Smith then asked the students to put down their pencils, and they spent some time discussing the review as well as what to expect over the next few days of class.

QUESTIONS

1. Why did Ms. Smith not just tell Jacob that you divide the numerator by the denominator? What did she do instead? What are some other things she could have done?

2. What interpretation of division did Ms. Smith use to help a student understand 3½ divided by ½? When the student had trouble, how did Ms. Smith use prior knowledge to help the student?

3. Should Ms. Smith be spending so much time on what were essentially review problems?

4. "Turned it into a decimal," "wrote it as a decimal," "changed it into what form?" are all phrases used in the scenario. Which of these might be problematic and why?

Commentary on Case 2: A Teacher Educator's Perspective

Lisa Boté

Although this lesson was meant to be a review of knowledge and skills, Ms. Smith moves the students forward in their understanding through the communication and use of student ideas. Understanding is multifaceted, including the ability to *explain* and *apply* (Wiggins and McTighe, 1998). Ms. Smith uses the meaningful context of shopping and sales tax to engage her students in the application of their knowledge of fractions, decimals, and percentages. In addition, Ms. Smith makes several requests throughout the lesson for students to explain their thinking and reasoning.

The idea that to understand something you must be able to use it is not a new one in education. For example, Bloom's taxonomy (1956) suggests application as central to understanding. Ms. Smith puts fractions, decimals, and percentages in a real-world context to give her students the opportunity to apply what they know. Without context, mathematics is reduced to procedures and closes the window to student understanding. Had Ms. Smith simply asked students to convert a fraction or multiply a whole number and decimal the students would simply learn, remember, and repeat/practice a procedure. In context, students must negotiate, adapt, and customize their knowledge in order to use it—thus opening the window to understanding.

If the application of knowledge opens the window to students' understanding, the request for explanation reveals their understanding. Understanding is not the mere knowledge of facts and procedures, but rather knowledge of why and how procedures work. Therefore, understanding can be revealed when we call on students to explain. It is Ms. Smith's request for explanation when she asks Jacob to "tell the class what he is doing as he writes" that reveals his understanding that .05 is equivalent to 5 percent and that the tax is an addition to the original cost of an item. Later a request for explanation reveals Jacob's misunderstanding about the procedure for converting a fraction to a decimal.

Understanding is always a matter of degree but can be moved forward through the use of ideas and the questions and discussion that arise. Without both application and explanation there is little opportunity for student understanding to be furthered. In addition, without both application and explanation teachers may have a false perception of students' understanding.

Case 3
Getting a Sense of Grams: Building Conceptual Understanding

Fourth-Grade Mathematics Lesson

CASE SETTING

Emma Hinton, a first-year teacher, taught this class at Brookfield Elementary School. Like the rest of her fourth-grade team, Ms. Hinton's classroom was in a portable outside the main building. This particular lesson occurred late in the morning toward the end of the school year. Of the twenty-four students in Ms. Hinton's class, 59 percent were or had been in the FARMs program, 27 percent were or had been in ESOL classes, and 18 percent currently or once had an IEP. The class was also culturally diverse: 41 percent of the students were Hispanic, 28 percent African American, 19 percent white, and 10 percent Asian. The focus of this hour-long lesson was mass and weight. After a whole group warm-up and review of the topic, the students quickly rearranged their desks to make six groups of four.

CASE OVERVIEW

The following excerpt is from a class where the teacher encouraged the students to use reasoning in order to understand and solve problems. The mathematical focus of the lesson was to extend the students' knowledge of the metric system by exploring the relationships between the size and mass of objects. Ms. Hinton made connections to prior lessons about capacity, and she made real-world connections by allowing the students to manipulate objects while they learned about mass and weight. She also posed questions about the difference between mass and weight, but did not force the students to come to a conclusion right away. This lesson is a precursor to lessons on converting units. The lesson included attention to the Grade 3 Common Core Standard that focuses on conceptual understanding of the units with which the students would be dealing.

RELATED COMMON CORE STATE STANDARD

Grade 3
Measurement and Data
Standard 2:

- Measure and estimate liquid volumes and masses of objects using standard units of grams (g), kilograms (kg), and liters (l); add, subtract, multiply, or divide to solve one-step word problems involving masses or volumes that are given in the same units, for example, by using drawings (such as a beaker with a measurement scale) to represent the problem.

THE CASE

The class began with a measurement warm-up where students had to choose a reasonable unit of measure or choose the best estimate for a given object. All warm-up questions dealt with capacity. After the warm-up, Ms. Hinton conducted a general review of metric measurement, including the metric prefixes, their abbreviations, and their meanings. Then she began the day's lesson.

"Today we're going to talk about mass," stated Ms. Hinton. She reminded the students that they had discussed weight in the prior week, and the students had wondered whether mass and weight were the same. Rather than solving the dilemma, Ms. Hinton reiterated that "today we're going to be working with mass." She reminded the students of a science experiment in which they had weighed bubble gum using a scale. She asked what unit of measure they had used. "Grams," said a student.

"Okay, grams." She requested that they add some notes to the chart they had been creating. She asked them to write the word "mass" underneath where they had written "capacity" and noted that the unit would be grams. "Now, I want you to think and predict. . . . I want you to predict what we call one thousand grams." A student suggested, "A kilogram." Ms. Hinton acknowledged the response and asked, "And how do you think we're going to abbreviate this?" Student answers varied, and Ms. Hinton clarified that "kg" was the correct abbreviation.

"What do you think I would call one-thousandth of a gram?" Ms. Hinton elaborated. "I have a gram and I'm going to break it into a thousand same-sized parts. What am I going to call that? Antonio?" The student suggested that it would be "an ounce." Ms. Hinton pointed out that an ounce was an English measurement and that the answer would have something to do with grams. "You don't have to guess," suggested Ms. Hinton. "One-thousandth of a gram is called what? Malad?" The student suggested it would be "a milligram."

"Milligram," repeated Ms. Hinton. She stated that they would be working with some objects and thinking about their mass. She went to her desk and picked up two objects. "Now, what are these?" A student noted that she was holding cereal boxes. After some discussion of the meaning of "attributes," Ms. Hinton asked for some attributes of the cereal boxes. Students suggested that they "taste good," they are "the same size," and they are "both cereals." Arzou suggested that "they have the same amount of cereal," but Tom disagreed, claiming that some boxes have more cereal in them than others.

When Ms. Hinton asked what the other students thought, Antonio suggested that they would "weigh about the same." Ms. Hinton said that the class was going to think about whether or not two things of the same size would weigh the same. She asked the students to arrange themselves in groups of four. There were six such groups.

After the students settled, Ms. Hinton told them that they "will be given several items . . . to compare their mass." Afterward, they would be given an "unknown" item and asked to estimate its mass. Ms. Hinton then gave each group a can of tuna and three other cans that varied in shape and weight. The students were given five minutes to look at the items and determine their mass.

When the class reconvened as a whole group, Ms. Hinton asked what they had learned. Arzou said that each can provided the number of grams it held, which he said would be the mass. "All right. How many grams [are] in the can that you're holding?" asked Ms. Hinton. Arzou said the can had 411 grams in it. Ayesha said that one of her cans held 170 grams. "Does that make sense?" asked Ms. Hinton. "Does that seem reasonable?" Although some students said that it was reasonable, Ayesha insisted that it was not.

Ms. Hinton asked Ayesha to elaborate on her response. "Why not? Why not, Ayesha?" The girl suggested that the can was not large enough to hold that many grams. Ms. Hinton told the class to hold the tuna can next to the large can at their table. Then she asked again, "Does it seem reasonable that that little can is 170 grams?" Elizabeth noted that the tuna can appeared to be about one-third the size of the large can. Ms. Hinton reminded the students that the large can had over 400 grams in it (although the large cans varied slightly from table to table). She then suggested they check Elizabeth's conjecture with some mental arithmetic. "And 170, what's 170 times 3? Do break apart. Hundred times three? 300. Seventy times three? 210. 300 plus 210? 510. Is 510 pretty close to the amount of the big can?" The students acknowledged that it was close.

Ms. Hinton continued, "All right. What did you notice about that little can?" Katie said that it held 79 grams. "Does that seem reasonable?" asked Ms. Hinton. "Compare it to the other cans you have. Does it seem reasonable? What do you think?" Some students said it was reasonable and others said it was not. Katie thought it was not reasonable, and Ms. Hinton asked her why she thought that. "Because that can doesn't look like it could hold 79 grams," claimed Katie.

Ms. Hinton asked Katie to compare the small can to the other tuna can. "How much is in that tuna can?" Katie said there were 175 grams in the larger can. "And what's the relationship . . . between the small can and the big can?" Ms. Hinton noted that the large can was about twice as big. She also noted that 79 was close to 80. "What's 80 times two? What's our basic fact? Eight times two is 16. Add a zero. 160." Ms. Hinton asked the class whether 170 and 160 were close to each other, and the class agreed that they were.

At this point, Ms. Hinton handed out the "unknown," which was a small clear bag containing brown rice. She told the class they would have one minute to estimate its mass. "What do you think you need to do?" she asked. "What are you going to do?" Bryant suggested they should "use these other things." Ms. Hinton asked him to elaborate. "How are you going to use those other things, Bryant?" The student noted that the small can weighed 170 grams. Ms. Hinton allowed the groups to work together for a minute but continued to ask, "How are you going to figure it out?"

When Ms. Hinton asked for estimates, students gave 255, 172, 177, and 200. Ms. Hinton stopped and asked the class, "When we did estimates with dollar amounts and stuff, did we ever come up with $2.43 for an estimate?" The students said they did not. "What [did] we always come up with, Brandon?" The student said "zero," but Ms. Hinton elaborated with "zero at the end." She pointed out that the last estimate did have a zero at the end, and she asked the first three groups if they wanted to revise their estimates. Their revised estimates were 250, 180, and 170.

Ms. Hinton reminded the students that estimates were not exact. "How are we going to find out exactly what it is?" she asked. "Weigh it," suggested a student. Ms. Hinton handed the groups small chips that weigh different amounts, but she noted that she did not have enough of them. "So what are we going to do?" One student suggested they use the cans. "Okay, responded Ms. Hinton. "I want you to get as close as you can with the materials you have in front of you. Then I'll allow you to add on with the weights I have."

As the groups worked, Ms. Hinton asked the students to tell her how many chips they thought they needed. She also asked the groups questions like, "Are you pretty close?" and "Did you try using the little can?" When the groups had finished, Ms. Hinton asked them how much their cans weighed. The groups seemed to agree with 200 grams. "Who was surprised with how much the rice weighed?" she asked. Harry said he thought it would have weighed more because "it feels heavier."

Ms. Hinton asked the students to hold the rice next to the medium can. "Do they look about the same?" Some students said "yes" while others said "no." Ms. Hinton responded, "No. Do they almost weigh the same?" Again, some students said "yes" while others said "no." Ms. Hinton responded, "Yes. All right. Let's go back to our cereal box. Antonio, what did you say about these cereals?" The student remembered his conjecture from earlier during the class; namely, that the cereals would have the same weight. Ms. Hinton asked the student to stand and hold the cereal boxes, one in each hand. "This weighs more," he said, indicating a particular box.

When asked how many grams were in each box of cereal, Antonio responded with 496 and 312. Ms. Hinton reminded the students that Tom had wondered if mass and weight were the same. "Do they look like they have the same mass?" Again, some students said "yes" while others said "no." Ms. Hinton continued, "Do they have the same weight?" All the students said "no." Ms. Hinton said that she would talk more about this, but for now, they had to put away their things and get ready to leave. She handed out the homework, which was similar to the warm-up questions except they involved mass instead of capacity. They were asked to choose a reasonable estimate for the mass of various objects. After a brief discussion, Ms. Hinton dismissed the class.

QUESTIONS

1. In what ways did Ms. Hinton engage the students in reasoning during the class?
2. Why did Ms. Hinton not let the students hold the cereal boxes at the beginning of the lesson? What would you have done in that situation?

3. What role did the cans play in the lesson? How might the lesson have changed if the cans were drawn and described on paper rather than manipulated by the students?

4. How did Ms. Hinton handle the issue of mass versus weight? Was her approach appropriate for fourth grade? Why or why not?

Commentary on Case 3: A Teacher Educator's Perspective

Lisa Boté

What struck me most in reading this case was the teacher questioning and its influence on student involvement. Ms. Hinton actively involved students in learning through not only the frequency of her questioning but also the type of questions asked. Ms. Hinton moves back and forth between queries evoking simple recall of information such as, "How much is in that tuna can?" or "What's 80 times 2?" and queries that request descriptions of thought processes such as "What are you going to do?" and "How are you going to use those other things?"

In addition, Ms. Hinton uses queries that evoke reflection on mathematical ideas and reflection on thought processes, thus engaging students in reasoning and metacognition. Being able to reason is essential to making sense of mathematics (NCTM, 1989). Reasoning is a habit of mind, and like all habits, it must be developed through consistent use (NCTM, 1989). Teacher questioning is one effective way to encourage and support student reasoning and independent learning.

When the function of a question or series of questions is to engage students in reasoning they need time to think—time to compose a response. It is difficult to discern, when reading this case, how much wait-time Ms. Hinton provided. Optimal wait-time varies with the question and the situation. However, research suggests that longer wait-times lead to higher quality student responses (Rowe, 1986). Nonetheless, Ms. Hinton clearly engages her students through the quantity, sequencing, and nature of her questions—all indications of effective lesson flow and clear goals (Good and Brophy, 2007).

Case 4

Converting among Customary Units of Measure: Attending to Students' Developmental Levels

Fifth-Grade Mathematics Lesson

CASE SETTING

A special education teacher, Evelyn Keller, taught this lesson at Brookfield Elementary School in the middle of April. It is the major part of the lesson that included Case 1. All of Ms. Keller's students had IEPs. This lesson focused on word problems that involved conversion between measurements.

CASE OVERVIEW

The following excerpt is from a class where special education students were engaged in high-level tasks such as

reasoning, explaining their thinking, and linking concepts
to procedures. The teacher exhibited the patience and
caring attitude that would be necessary to engage this
population of students in such tasks. The excerpt also
demonstrates the way a teacher can break such tasks into
smaller pieces without turning them into low-level tasks.
Although both Case 4 and Case 5 address the same Grade
5 Common Core Standard, the lessons illustrate quite
different approaches. In this case Ms. Keller emphasizes
the Standard of Mathematical Practice, "make sense of
problems and persevere in solving them," by ensuring
that her students understand the conversion problem and
keeping them focused on solving a problem. In Case 5,
Mr. Forrest includes conversion of units, but does so in
a larger context of problem solving by use of strategies
and resources.

RELATED COMMON CORE STATE STANDARD

Grade 5
Measurement and Data
Standard 1:

- Convert among different-sized standard measurement units
  within a given measurement system (e.g., convert 5 cm to 0.05
  m); and use these conversions in solving multistep, real-world
  problems.

THE CASE

During a lesson on conversions, Ms. Keller helped her students understand how to get started on a problem about milkshakes. She began by reading the problem to the students. "What if Al had twenty-three milkshake orders and three gallons of milk? Would he have enough milk for one pint in each milkshake?" She pointed out that the question also asked for the students to explain their answers. She said that they were going to work on strategies for writing clear explanations.

"First, determine what . . . we know," she said. "What can you tell me about that problem? Give me some information from the problem." Rather than providing information from the problem, a student offered a strategy. "You could draw a picture." Ms. Keller went with it. "Okay, twenty-three milkshake orders. I could draw twenty-three milkshakes. It would take a little bit of time so I'm just going to . . . write twenty-three milkshakes." She proceeded to draw a picture of a can and labeled it "23 milkshakes."

Ms. Keller continued. "What other information do we know?" A student responded, "It says twenty-three gallons of milk." Ms. Keller asked a question in return. "Does it say twenty-three gallons of milk or does it say three gallons of milk?" The student corrected herself. "Three gallons." Ms. Keller agreed and drew three gallons of milk on the board.

"What else do we know from information in the story?" asked Ms. Keller. "There's one other important piece of information we need." A few students became distracted with drawing twenty-three cups and worrying about how pints are related to cups, but Ms. Keller refocused them. "Let's look at the problem. . . . Jervon, I need you to look at the problem and tell me what's the other important piece of information that's in the story? You don't need to spend all your time drawing that. If we spent all of our time drawing very fancy milkshakes we're not going to get to the math part of the problem, okay? Look at the problem. . . . What's the other important information from there? André?"

Ms. Keller decided to open a chart on the board that showed customary capacity units. Cups to pints to gallons were shown graphically. She then restated her request. "I want you to tell me, what's the other piece of information that we need to know that the story told us?" A student offered "one pint." Ms. Keller questioned the brief answer. "One pint what? What does that mean, one pint? What's the one pint mean?" The student said that there were twenty-three milkshakes to make. Ms. Keller asked again, "So the one pint tells us . . . ?" Finally, the student said, "How much you need."

Ms. Keller reiterated this point and then continued. "How much goes in each milkshake. So each milkshake has one pint. Okay. . . . What are the two units of measurement we have to think about? Jervon?" The student responded with "inches and feet." Ms. Keller asked the student if there were inches and feet in the story. "What are they talking about in here?" Several other students said "gallons," but Ms. Keller insisted that Jervon answer. "Gallons," he said.

"Gallons and pints," added Ms. Keller. "We have pints and we've got gallons. Now is a good time to go and look at the picture and look at gallons and look at pints. He's got how many gallons of milk?" Several students answered with "three." Ms. Keller then pointed to the picture to illustrate the three gallons. She also reminded the students that they were asked to decide whether or not there would be enough milk for the milkshakes and that they needed to explain their answer.

"In your explanation I have to be able to see not just a yes or no if he could make those milkshakes. I've got to be able to tell from either the words, numbers, or pictures, or a combination of those, on your paper how you arrived at your yes he can do it or no he can't do it. Okay?" After answering a few more questions, Ms. Keller asked the students to begin working on the problem.

QUESTIONS

1. What did Ms. Keller do to help the students understand the milkshake problem? Do you feel she lowered the level of the task? Provide evidence for your answer.
2. How did Ms. Keller handle incorrect or inappropriate answers? Do you agree with the way she handled them?
3. Imagine Ms. Keller posing a follow-up problem. How should her scaffolding of this new problem compare to the scaffolding she provided for the milkshake problem? Should she provide the same level of support? More? Less? Why?

Commentary on Case 4:
A Teacher's Perspective

Christine Peterson Tardif

High expectations for all students and differentiating to help students meet curriculum requirements can go hand in hand. Students who have learning disabilities or behavior difficulties are just as capable of exploring math concepts if their needs are met while challenging their minds to extend. Ms. Keller keeps the students on track during the lesson so that wondering minds do not waste precious time.

This was a small class, but even a larger class could have the same effect with group work or with coteaching. Using formative assessments to evaluate the needs of the students could help with grouping to meet their needs. Use an exit card with a question or problem from that day's lesson. Sort the cards into groups for the next day (i.e., got it, almost there, need review). The next day you could scaffold for the students according to their needs, but by working in groups you can do it in less time. If you are fortunate enough to have a coteacher please take advantage of it! Coteaching can involve another general education teacher, a specialist (reading, math), or a special educator. Planning together and making sure that the students understand that both teachers are equal in the classroom and both are responsible for all the students are essential to making a coteaching classroom work.

The beginning of the lesson is an excellent time to review capacity equivalent measures as a warm-up to the lesson. This will help the students connect to past knowledge that they need to activate in the day's lesson; it also allows the teacher to see what may need to be reviewed prior to the lesson. Also a review of the types of measurements would be helpful here. Use a chart that was generated with the students when learning each type of measurement (e.g., capacity, linear, weight, time) and focus the students' thinking on the correct type.

I love the idea of drawing a picture to explain math thinking. This is so important for students. Making a picture helps them visualize abstract concepts and assists them in explaining their thinking, not only to others but to themselves as well.

Case 5
Converting Units within
a System of Measurement:
Encouraging Resourcefulness

Fifth-Grade Mathematics Lesson

CASE SETTING

This lesson was taught by Richard Forrest, who was in his third year of teaching. The lesson took place at Orchard Creek Elementary School in late spring from 10:20 to 11:30. The room was large, with a number of bookshelves holding textbooks and library books. There were several bulletin boards, one showing stem and leaf plots, apparently drawn by the students. Mr. Forrest had fifteen students for math, of whom nearly half were currently in or had recently exited from ESOL classes; over half the students were or had been in the FARMs program. The class was also culturally diverse: six students were Hispanic, three African American, three white, and two Asian. Students' desks were arranged in clusters, with four clusters of four desks and one of five desks. The students were quiet and reserved as Mr. Forrest began the day's lesson on measurement conversion strategies.

CASE OVERVIEW

The lesson involved explicit discussion of strategies. The teacher made connections to the real world to help students understand how and when strategies are used. Mr. Forrest explained in an interview after the lesson that he focused heavily on skills and strategies because his students often told him, "When I get out of school, I'll never have to see math again. It will be gone. I won't have to deal with it." Mr. Forrest emphasized that "in our lives every day from the minute we wake up to the minute we go to sleep, there's a strategy, there's a skill involved. It's a mix of things" (interview). The mathematical purpose of the lesson was for the students to use conversions as a strategy for either pairing or ordering various measurements. The students were encouraged to use a variety of resources and skills to complete the tasks. Although both Case 5 and Case 4 address the same Grade 5 Common Core Standard, the lessons illustrate quite different approaches. In this case, Mr. Forrest includes conversion of units, but does so in a larger context of problem solving by use of strategies and resources. In Case 4, Ms. Keller emphasizes the Standard of Mathematical Practice, "make sense of problems and persevere in solving them," by ensuring that her students understand the conversion problem and keeping them focused on solving a problem.

RELATED COMMON CORE STATE STANDARD

Grade 5
Measurement and Data
Standard 1:

- Convert among different-sized standard measurement units within a given measurement system (e.g., convert 5 cm to 0.05 m); and use these conversions in solving multistep, real-world problems.

THE CASE

Near the beginning of the lesson, Mr. Forrest walked to the chalkboard at the front of the room and wrote "Strategy." He then asked a student, "What does it mean to use a strategy? It could be reading or math or anything else. When people use the word strategy, what do they mean?" A student responded with "ways to help them." Another student suggested it was "something you already know." Mr. Forrest asked for clarification. "Something you know already, like background knowledge?"

After listing these ideas on the board, Mr. Forrest asked, "What does a strategy help you do?" A student suggested that "it helps you answer a question." Another responded that is helps make a task easier, and another said it is something you do to help you figure something out. Mr. Forrest added these ideas to the list on the board and then asked how a strategy might be used outside of school. He paused and offered a scenario. "Okay, how about this?

How about your mom or dad is driving somewhere and there's a huge accident. They come to an intersection and there's an accident. Everything's blocked off. What strategy might they use?" A student suggested they could go a different way.

Mr. Forrest offered another scenario. "How about if you need to buy clothing and you don't quite have enough money to buy what you really want, what strategy might you use?" A girl suggested buying something cheaper. "That's one strategy," said Mr. Forrest. Another student said to put the item on lay-away. Mr. Forrest was enthusiastic, "Good! That's another strategy; people use it all the time. Good. What else? What other strategies do people use? I might wait for what?" One student said to wait for a sale.

"So these are all different things that we do," Mr. Forrest said. "It's not just reading and math and school, but it's everything we do all the time, is a strategy, okay? Now, tell me about math skills that you might use to answer a question. Skills—not strategies, but skills!" Mr. Forrest elicited a few skills, such as subtraction, multiplication, and finding equivalent values. The students also suggested that being able to use mathematical tools, such as protractors, calculators, rulers, and computers, was a skill. Mr. Forrest then began to prepare the students for an activity. He stated that they "may use any skill, any strategy, any material, any resource to help you come to your final answer and do what you think is the right way to do it. There's no limitation within the classroom."

Mr. Forrest explained that the students would be organized into four groups, each with a different task to complete. On a card, the students of each group were to write down any strategy, skill, or materials they used to complete the task. When prompted, the students quietly and quickly got into their groups and began to work. Each group was given a set of cards containing a variety of units of measurement and was either to pair the cards or put them in order, and the groups worked on their tasks for about fifteen minutes.

As the groups worked, Mr. Forrest encouraged them with words but did very little to assist. He praised one group by saying, "That's a smart strategy, to use a sticky note." He suggested to another group that if they were struggling, they could discuss it with the whole class when it was their turn to present the solution to their task. Mr. Forrest said they were "going to discuss the different strategies that you could have used in order to answer the questions."

Before allowing the groups to present their solutions, Mr. Forrest asked the students about the task difficulty. "Hard activity? Easy activity? Medium activity?" The students' answers varied and Mr. Forrest asked, "Why do we all have a different view on whether it's easy or hard?" One student suggested they each have different knowledge. Another suggested, "We don't know how to do things in the same way." Other suggestions were that the activities might not be the same, some students may not be used to the topic, and that people think differently. Mr. Forrest seemed to like this response, replying, "We think differently. Our brains work differently. Good. And skills and strategies help us do things. In life, in math, in traffic, at our jobs, in college, when we go shopping, everything we do." He then posed another (nonmathematical) dilemma and asked what strategy the students would use in the situation. The students suggested four different strategies.

Mr. Forrest explained to the class that the primary purpose of the activity had been to practice and apply the concept of equivalence. He asked, "Why did I tell you to use resources, every resource you could think about—Patricia?" Patricia suggested that the resources could help them answer the questions.

As each group explained their task and solutions, Mr. Forrest asked them how they knew when two things were equivalent. The first group to share had been asked to organize their cards into pairs. They created the following pairs: 5 cm = 50 mm, 18 in = half yard, 12 qt = 3 gal, 0.1 m = 10 cm, and ¾ ft = 9 in. The students explained most of the pairs using basic conversions. For example, they said that 10 millimeters was the same as 1 centimeter and 1 yard equals 36 inches. When the students did not readily give one of the conversions, Mr. Forrest asked, "Do you remember how many quarts are in one gallon?"

Mr. Forrest asserted that the students had used what he called "equivalents" to pair their cards. He also pointed to other prior knowledge involved in the task, such as their knowledge of decimals and fractions. "So you're going back to equivalents, you're going back to fractions, you're going back to—do you see all these skills that are building, the background knowledge, how important it is?"

During another group's explanation, Mr. Forrest commented that the students had not paired the cards as he expected, but "every single [pairing] made sense to me because you explained it correctly." In the case of this group, the students used various attributes to pair their items. One student explained, "For example, this one we looked at the units." The student was describing a pair that involved square units. "Square units," replied Mr. Forrest. "Very good. Excellent."

He continued to emphasize the importance of student's explanations and the strategies they used. One group that had to order their numbers from largest to smallest said that they used a measurement fact sheet, ruler, and calculator to help them with their task. Mr. Forrest added to their list of strategies by suggesting they used a very important strategy to get started; namely, they were careful to read the instructions and make sure they understood what was being asked of them. He noted that sometimes students order numbers from smallest to largest because they do not read the directions carefully. He also remarked that "they started in their minds maybe with the smallest, even though that was going to be the last one."

After inspecting their list, Mr. Forrest noted two mistakes. The first mistake was placing 5 km after 2,000 m. Mr. Forrest resolved the issue using equivalents. "How many meters are in a kilometer?" he asked. The second mistake was placing ½ km after 3 m. Mr. Forrest asked the same question in response to this mistake and added, "What's half of a thousand?" Because the group had incorrectly ordered two of their measurements, Mr. Forrest asked the students what would have made the task easier for them. A student suggested that it would have helped if the resource sheet had more equivalents on it. Apparently, the students had known they needed equivalents to help order the cards, even though they had struggled with a few of the measurements.

The class ended with the students taking a short quiz on measurement. "Any resource you want to use is fine," instructed Mr. Forrest, "but remember, keep in mind you have only ten minutes." The quiz was similar in nature to the group activity including an item that was one of the tasks the class had just reviewed, but now the students were directed that they must work "100 percent independently."

QUESTIONS

1. What is a "strategy," according to Mr. Forrest? Would you add anything to his definition? How does his notion of strategy differ from the usual notion of strategies for mathematical problem solving?
2. What role did strategy play in the lesson? What role did equivalents play in the lesson?
3. Why did Mr. Forrest not reveal the purpose of the lesson until after the students had completed the tasks?
4. How did Mr. Forrest respond the first time a group did not complete the task as expected? How did this response differ from his response the second time a group did not complete the task as expected? What would you have done in each of these cases?
5. What rationale might Mr. Forrest have had to include one of the lesson tasks as an item on the quiz?

Commentary on Case 5: An English for Speakers of Other Languages (ESOL) Perspective

Rebecca Oxford and Min-tun Chuang

Mr. Forrest's instruction emphasized some important notions: strategies and student differences. In a very diverse class, or in any class for that matter, it is important to help students realize that people use strategies as tools to solve problems and that the strategies they employ often differ across students. Mr. Forrest successfully demystified the concept of strategies, making it more concrete for the students in the class. Similarly, Oxford (1990, 1996) and Lan and Oxford (2003) emphasize that within a group, as well as across ethnic and linguistic groups, there are differences in strategies used by individuals.

Mr. Forrest seemed sensitive to students' individual differences and wanted them to understand as well. The tasks he used to get this message across were very relevant.

He could have gone further by emphasizing the strategic nature of several of the students' own behaviors: using equivalents and drawing on prior knowledge. This would have strengthened and deepened the students' understanding of strategies. Perhaps he was trying not to give too many examples, or perhaps he simply did not recognize these opportunities.

Given the large proportion of students in the class who were learning English as their second language, Mr. Forrest could have mentioned that different *groups*, not just different individual students, sometimes use different strategies for solving problems. He could have mentioned that children in the United States and Mexico are taught different ways to solve long-division problems (H. C. Stocking, personal communication, January 2004) or that because Japanese students receive extensive abacus training, they transfer their specific calculation strategies to pencil-and-paper math problems (Hatano, 1982). He could have asked the children in the class from other countries whether they noticed any differences in math strategies in the United States as compared to their home countries. Naturally, in any such discussion he would need to avoid any firm cultural stereotyping, because there is always within-group variation, even within a given culture. (Additional resources about culturally influenced math strategies include *Ethnomathematics* [Ascher, 1991] and *The Handbook of Cross-Cultural Psychology* [Matsumoto, 2001].)

Case 6
Distinguishing between Area and Perimeter: Using Multiple Representations to Aid Discrimination

Fifth-Grade Mathematics Lesson

CASE SETTING

This class was taught by Greta Shepard, a veteran of forty years, at Hawthorne Elementary School early in the spring semester. It was a fifth-grade intervention class that supplemented regular classroom instruction for small groups of students who were having difficulty with a particular topic. Meeting for a half-hour in the morning, the class typically provided either a preview of or follow-up to the daily math lesson. Ten students were in class that day, six girls and four boys. Most were Hispanic, with a few African American and white students also receiving this extra assistance. In addition to being the intervention teacher, Ms. Shepard provided resource help to classroom teachers. Her intervention classes met at round tables in her spacious resource room, which was filled with mathematics books and materials. The topic for the day was perimeter.

RELATED COMMON CORE STATE STANDARD

Grade 4
Measurement and Data
Standard 3:

- Apply the area and perimeter formulas for rectangles in real world and mathematical problems. *For example, find the width of a rectangular room given the area of the flooring and the length, by viewing the area formula as a multiplication equation with an unknown factor.*

CASE OVERVIEW

The following excerpt is from a lesson on perimeter. Ms. Shepard used contexts and models to help students understand why adding each side of a rectangle would give the distance around its outside edge. Previously in this class they worked on area. During this lesson, Ms. Shepard explicitly contrasted area with perimeter to help students overcome some common misconceptions.

THE CASE

The class began with a review of the previous day's lesson. Ms. Shepard asked the students to find the area of a rectangle that was 45 meters long and 23 meters wide. As she moved around the room to observe the students working, she asked questions like, "What do you remember about area?" When a boy stated that it had something to do with length and width, she asked, "Okay, but what operation? Add, subtract, multiply, or divide?"

Ms. Shepard returned to the front of the class and asked the group some similar questions. After the class established that area was equal to length times width, she wrote A = L × W on the overhead. She then asked for the product and the appropriate units. Afterward, Ms. Shepard asked students to sketch the rectangle on their papers, as she modeled on the overhead. She questioned them about labeling the sketch, including which sides would be 45 meters and why. Included in this discussion was the fact that opposite sides of a rectangle are the same length.

Although the students had already calculated the area, Ms. Shepard pointed to the inside of the rectangle she drew on the overhead and asked, "Okay. Children, if the area is 1,035 meters [squared], please tell me what would be in here if I had you draw it?" The students were easily able to tell her there would be 1,035 squares. "Would you like to do that?" she asked. The students agreed that they would not want to draw all the squares.

At this point, Ms. Shepard began to contrast what would be inside the rectangle with what the outer edge would be. "Now, look at my rectangle that I've sketched.

Suppose this was a garden and I have a lot of carrots in that garden. And rabbits came and ate my carrots so I decided to put up a fence around my garden because the rabbits come in and the deer come in at night. What part of that rectangle would I take to fence?" A student offered that the fence should go "around the whole thing." Ms. Shepard asked the students to use a red pen to illustrate the fence using the sketch on their papers.

One student used the term "perimeter" and Ms. Shepard repeated it. "Perimeter. Okay. The perimeter is the outside edge. Children, now I need your attention up here. Did we draw squares when we traced the outside of this garden? What did we draw?" The students were uncertain, so Ms. Shepard elaborated on her question. She traced an edge of a square and asked, "What am I drawing? From here to here, what am I drawing?" A student finally said that the teacher had drawn a line. She accepted this response, but not without clarification. "Exactly. Just a line, or a line segment?" She continued, saying "I did not draw squares . . . to find the perimeter."

Ms. Shepard then instructed the students to take ten square tiles from the basket in front of them and use them to create a rectangle. After examining their work, she created the same rectangle on the overhead by using transparent tiles. The rectangle was made of five tiles along one side and two tiles along the other.

She then asked the students to tell her "without counting, without calculating, with just thinking, what's the area of this rectangle? What's the area of this rectangle? Kaye?" A girl said the area was ten, and Ms. Shepard asked, "Why is it ten?" The teacher made the point that the students "took out ten squares and the area is always the squares in the middle. . . . So it has to be ten [squared]."

Ms. Shepard returned to the discussion about perimeter. "But I want to know what the perimeter is right now. . . . Now, I'm only talking about the outside edge. . . . I'm only talking about the outside edge. I want you to count each section up here of the outside edge. Go ahead and count it." Ms. Shepard worked with the students until each side of the rectangle was labeled.

Then Ms. Shepard asked, "What was the area again?" Several students replied, "Ten." She reminded the students of the area formula the students had given her. "And what is five times two?" she asked. The students again replied, "Ten." Ms. Shepard repeated their answer but pointed out it was "not going to be the perimeter." Finally, she requested, "Tell me how I can get that entire outside edge for that fence?"

Rather than accepting answers immediately, Ms. Shepard asked the students to talk with someone at their table about the problem. Meanwhile, she observed what the students were doing and asked questions to guide them. One student looked confused, and Ms. Shepard suggested that she did not "have to add, subtract, multiply, or divide." She said, "Just do something and tell me what the outside edge is."

One student suggested they could measure the rectangle, but Ms. Shepard suggested they did not have anything to measure it with. She followed this response by asking the students what they could do if they had to find the length without measuring.

At this point, Ms. Shepard gained the class's attention. "Okay, everybody watch up here. . . . I want you to watch.

I'm not going to add. I'm not going to subtract. I'm not going to multiply. I'm not going to divide." She began to count, "One, two, three, four, five, six, seven, eight, nine, ten, eleven, twelve, thirteen, fourteen. What did I do?"

A student suggested that the teacher had just counted. Ms. Shepard reiterated this point and restated the total. "Fourteen. I got fourteen. Now, some kids get confused here. Some kids say that you count squares." She continued, "I've got ten squares here, don't I? But my answer is fourteen. So I don't have fourteen squares, do I? No. I haven't added any squares." Ms. Shepard made the point that she only counted the outside edge. Then she asked, "Can I do anything mathematically with these numbers and come up with fourteen? Can I add, subtract, multiply, or divide and come up with fourteen?" A student suggested that the sides could be added.

Seemingly pleased, Ms. Shepard asked the students to take two more squares from the basket. As she constructed a 4 × 3 rectangle on the overhead, she asked the students to do the same. When they were ready, she said, "I have to check out this adding the sides thing because I'm not sure. I think that was a good idea but I have to be sure. I got to check out. I have to experiment more than once. Right now, children, please go around and count the outside edge."

Three students gave fourteen as their answer, while two gave eleven. Ms. Shepard responded by saying, "Let's check it out, okay. Everybody look up here with me. [I am] just going to count the outside edge." She requested that the students count along with her. As they did, Ms. Shepard marked off each section as they completed it.

After they finished counting, she asked, "Kristen, tell me, what strategy did I use to make sure I didn't count . . . one of the sections . . . more than once. What did I do? What did you just see me do so I didn't keep on counting?"

Ms. Shepard then asked the students to sketch a rectangle and label the sides four, three, four, and three. "Now, you told me before if I added up all four sides I would get the perimeter. What do we already know the perimeter is?" The students said the perimeter was fourteen. Then Ms. Shepard asked the students to add all the sides on paper. "I need to see your addition," she said. Observing their work, the teacher complimented a student on the grouping strategy she used. Then she said, "Raise your hand and tell me, what sum did you get when you added up all four sides?" The students all got fourteen. "So do you think that worked?" The students agreed that it did.

Ms. Shepard had the students complete one more example, both by counting and by adding. She encouraged them to use a strategy when they counted the edges. All students agreed on the answer. She then asked the students how many squares the rectangle was composed of, what its area was, and what operation they used to get the area. They contrasted area with perimeter, stating that one involved multiplication and one involved addition. She then pointed out that both involve a formula and wrote $P = S + S + S + S$ on the overhead.

Ms. Shepard concluded the lesson by having the students try four examples. They were allowed to use calculators to complete these examples, but Ms. Shepard asked that they still write the addition problem on their papers. After they finished, she asked them to write a formula for finding the perimeter of a rectangle. She stated, "It can be in words. It could be a formula. How do you find the perimeter of a rectangle?" After one minute, Ms. Shepard asked the students to gather their belongings. As they did this, she had a student verbalize how to find the perimeter of a rectangle. A girl stated that adding all the numbers along the sides would give the perimeter. Ms. Shepard approved, and the students formed a line and exited the room.

QUESTIONS

1. Why did Ms. Shepard spend so much time having students find area and perimeter without using a formula?

2. Name at least three different representations Ms. Shepard used to show perimeter. What benefit might the multiple representations have?

3. Ms. Shepard had the students find the perimeter of the 4 × 3 rectangle in more than one way. What purpose did this serve?

4. One of the students in this class wrote: "Add the area to get the answer" when asked to write how to find the perimeter. What was this student thinking? How would you respond?

Case 7
Exploring the Meanings of "Volume": Recognizing a Word's Everyday Meaning and Its Mathematical Meaning

Fifth-Grade Mathematics Lesson

CASE SETTING

Jason DiLoretto, in his sixteenth year of teaching, taught this lesson at Ella Flagg Elementary School on a morning in late spring. The teacher described the twenty-three students in the class as being low to average in math. One of the students was or had been in ESOL, two students once or currently had an IEP, and five (22 percent) were or had been FARMs. Although the school was in a distant suburb, the student population was culturally diverse: 35 percent of the students were African

American, 30 percent Hispanic, 22 percent white, and 13 percent Asian. Students were seated at individual adjoining desks that created four long horizontal rows facing the front of the room. The lesson focused on attributes of a triangle and volume of a rectangular prism. On the board was the objective: Develop and use formulas to determine the volume of rectangular prisms.

CASE OVERVIEW

The following excerpt is from a class in which the teacher attempted to help students understand mathematical concepts by making connections to the real world. In particular, the teacher wanted the students to understand "attributes" and "volume." The intent of the scenario is to illustrate ways that this teacher used real-world connections for the purpose of scaffolding. The lesson also indicated his awareness that everyday meanings could hinder as well as facilitate understanding of mathematical terms.

RELATED COMMON CORE STATE STANDARD

Grade 5
Measurement and Data
Standard 3:

- Recognize volume as an attribute of solid figures and understand concepts of volume measurement.

THE CASE

Mr. DiLoretto began the class by stating that they were going to continue Thursday's lesson about attributes. Over the weekend, students were to have asked their parents about their "attributes." Sophia provided the first list, which included words like loving, honest, hard working, and responsible. Mr. DiLoretto asked Sophia whether or not her parents knew what attributes were. "They knew," she said.

Mr. DiLoretto then asked another student to share a list. The next student's list included words like kind, funny, loving, and honest. "Did she know what attributes were?" asked Mr. DiLoretto. "I had to explain to her a little bit," said the student.

Mr. DiLoretto continued having students share. The next list included words like helpful, noisy, and hardworking. Mr. DiLoretto pointed out that he was "hearing some of the same attributes." Then he asked the student, "Your parents are noisy?" The student replied, "Yeah, they are noisy!"

Mr. DiLoretto then switched the conversation to attributes of a triangle. "Who would like to come up to the board and put one of those attributes of a triangle up on the board?" About five students raise their hands. "I should see hands popping up. . . . Come up and help me at the board." Mr. DiLoretto went to the board and wrote "Attributes of a Triangle." As he wrote, he said the words aloud. He then asked the students to lower their hands so they could review the definition. "What are attributes?" asked Mr. DiLoretto.

While standing, a student defined an attribute as "a quality or a characteristic" and then he wrote "three sides" on the board. "That's a good start. . . . Very good. We are going back to our geometry unit, back in Unit Two. Who else?" Another student recalled that the sum of the angles in a triangle equals 180 degrees. Mr. DiLoretto responded, "Very nice. Where did you get that from?" The student stated that the fact was from a study sheet Mr. DiLoretto had given them. Mr. DiLoretto seemed impressed. "Notes from the past?" he asked. "Excellent. Good job. I like the way you are organized and you went back and reviewed your notes."

Another student stated that triangles have three vertices. Mr. DiLoretto asked the student to give another name for vertices. When the student said "corners," Mr. DiLoretto responded, "Fantastic. Who else has any other attributes of a triangle? You guys are beginning to understand what attributes are all about. You can figure out what your own attributes are . . . Sophia, do you have another one? Come on up, my friend."

Later during the class, Mr. DiLoretto shifted the focus to volume of a rectangular prism. "Now that you know what attributes are . . . you're now going to find the volume of rectangular prisms." He then drew a very clear and accurate rectangular prism on the board and labeled the dimensions as 5 cm × 6 cm × 8 cm. Mr. DiLoretto told the students the formula for finding volume and wrote $V = l \times w \times h$ on the board. He also reminded the students that during Thursday's lesson on attributes, they had discussed length and width.

Mr. DiLoretto asked for the length of the rectangular prism on the board, but he quickly changed his focus to the concept of volume when he realized the students were confused. "I am looking out there and I'm not even sure people know what volume is. . . . What is volume? Is it the button you press on the tape recorder to turn up the music? Isn't that volume? When we are talking about volume in math, what are we referring to?"

Mr. DiLoretto praised the students who were paying attention and then continued. "We don't really know what volume is, do we? Just like we didn't know what attributes were last Thursday." He assured them it was okay and that they would know the definition before they left the class. Mr. DiLoretto gave a formal definition and wrote it on the board as he spoke. "Volume is the amount of space a solid figure occupies." He then acknowledged that the students may not understand it yet. "We put a lot of words on the chalkboard, but what does it mean? Look at where you are sitting right now. Your desk. Does that have a volume? Is it a solid figure? Is it taking up space?"

Mr. DiLoretto gave another example. "How about this book? Solid figure? Takes up space?" He stated that they could find the volume by measuring its length, width, and height and multiplying them together. Then Mr. DiLoretto asked the students to give some examples of their own. One student suggested that a door would have volume. "Absolutely. That's good, Shelise. . . . A door definitely would have volume." Other students suggested a fan, bulletin board, binder and computer as objects with volume. Mr. DiLoretto then asked if they were beginning to understand volume, before returning to a discussion about the formula.

Near the end of class, Mr. DiLoretto began summarizing the lesson. "Today in math, we continued what we started on Thursday. Learning what attributes are all about. You identified some of your parents' [attributes]. Some of my attributes. Attributes of a square. Rectangle. Triangle." He pointed out that they did not have a chance to share their own attributes, but they would do so before leaving. First, he wanted to summarize what was new for the day. "We took the next step. We went beyond attributes and today we began to find volume of rectangular prisms."

Mr. DiLoretto then asked a student to define volume and asked for some more examples of objects with volume. "A book," said one student. "A rectangular prism," said another student. Mr. DiLoretto also asked a student to give the formula for finding volume of a rectangular prism. Finally, he returned to personal attributes.

"Who can tell me some of your attributes?" asked Mr. DiLoretto. A few students responded, using words like "funny, smart, and kind" and "nice, playful, and helpful." Mr. DiLoretto then dismissed the class, wishing them a "wonderful day of learning" as they left the room.

QUESTIONS

1. Why is it important to connect mathematical ideas to everyday experiences?
2. What words did you have trouble with in math class? What are some other examples of terms such as volume that have common meanings that may interfere with students' understanding of their technical meaning in mathematics?
3. How would you help students make sense of those words?

Commentary on Case 7: An English for Speakers of Other Languages (ESOL) Perspective

Rebecca Oxford

The teacher, Mr. DiLoretto, was expert in taking a potentially very abstract topic and making it more student-friendly, familiar, and personal. It was quite useful for him to ask students to talk to their parents about human attributes before having the students discuss geometric attributes in class. When introducing volume of a geometric object, he laughingly joked about the volume on students' tape recorders to ensure that they knew that the topic of today's lesson was a *different* kind of volume. Much research (e.g., Ausubel, 1960; Mayer, 2002, 2003; Woolfolk, 2001) reveals that students can learn better when they start with something relatively familiar as an advance organizer before moving to new material or abstractions.

This teacher also recognized and supported students' affective needs at the same time as he addressed cognitive topics. He did this in several ways. First, by means of the weekend homework assignment he put students in the position of experts, explaining something to their parents while asking their parents for input. This was a deft affective move, elevating students from the status of feeling ignorant to the status of being knowledgeable. Second, when he asked students to come to the board, he did it by saying, "Come help me," playing down his own status as the expert and showing belief in the students' high capabilities, and "Come on up, my friend," indicating cordiality and friendship.

Third, he used praise often but sincerely, as in "Excellent. Good job. I like the way you are organized . . . ," and spoke encouragingly, as in "You guys are beginning to understand what attributes are. You can figure out what your own attributes are." Fourth, when students seemed puzzled about the volume of a rectangular prism, he moved back to a topic that he knew they could handle before moving on, so they would be both cognitively grounded and affectively supported. Fifth, he "bookended" the class, starting it off with the discussion about personal attributes and coming back to the same topic at the end, then wishing the group a "wonderful day of learning."

In short, Mr. DiLoretto showed a profound understanding of the cognitive requirements of his students and also of these children's emotional and motivational needs (see Brophy [2004] and Stipek [2001] on children's academic motivation).

Commentary on Case 7: A Teacher's Perspective

Christine Peterson Tardif

I love that Mr. DiLoretto talks about reading in math. It makes the student understand that he sees these subjects connected and a part of our real world together, even if at the moment it is the real world of the school day. Mr. DiLoretto is able to connect reading and math to help the students make links that will assist them to fully understand new concepts. This act of connecting, for me, is so important for the elementary student. It is difficult for them to compartmentalize things. We see this exemplified in our students every day. They can't forget that their cat ran away and need to talk about it throughout the day. They had a great time at recess and can't sit down and read silently for independent reading. They can't concentrate on the lesson when they are thinking about the argument they just had with the teacher or a friend. As adults we work hard at keeping ideas separate and unrelated. What children do is much more natural. I strongly disagree with the compartmentalization of elementary schools, although I realize that scheduling requirements may make it necessary. We should keep the elementary schoolteacher instructing most subjects to their students, not only math or reading or science. The teacher who teaches all the subjects to their students will be able to make the logical connections that the students will be able to use immediately. (In another lesson, for example, Ms. Hinton helps her students make connections in math by using a recent science experiment.)

Mr. DiLoretto has an excellent reading lesson on character traits included in the text. Here he connects to the math discussion. This is not a coming full circle as it first appears, but a building of a massive structure that has a firm base and supports to every part of the building. He goes back to connecting character traits and attributes from the other direction, reading to math. Character traits are difficult for students to identify. Use yourself to have students describe you (i.e., tall, brown hair, male) and connect these descriptions to attributes. Then have students talk about your personality (i.e., tough, friendly, helpful) and make the distinction that these are character traits. Have students note differences to help them keep them straight. Character traits can change but very slowly over time—or as the result of an important event (another connection to reading: cause/effect).

During the lesson Mr. DiLoretto moves on to the concept of volume. Because there is a big switch from attributes to volume, these concepts could have been two separate lessons. Although volume is certainly an attribute of geometric shapes, Mr. DiLoretto could have made that connection more explicit for his students. Or, he could have introduced the concept of volume as a preview for the next lesson, connecting it to perimeter and area, as well as attributes.

Note taking is a skill that needs to be taught to young students and Mr. DiLoretto teaches it well. It was great to have students use the resources that he gave them or that they generate in this lesson. Those class notes should be living documents to the students that are used and added to often. Another wonderful teaching moment came when a student used the term "vertices" when giving a description. Like Mr. DiLoretto, we should be sure to praise students for using math vocabulary. This can then be incorporated in a writing lesson to teach students that word choice is an important trait for good writers. Choosing vocabulary that is exactly what you want to say, whether it be a math term or a describing word, is a concept that students need to explore, practice, and transfer to their daily writing. It helps to communicate precisely what you are thinking to your reader.

Near the end of the lesson, Mr. DiLoretto is teaching the concept of volume. Here is an idea that I have used for teaching dimensions and volume and connecting to measurement: Use a throwaway plastic container with removable lid. Make sure the container is clear so students can see the interior. Trace one edge of the lid. Ask students what this is (a line). This is one dimension, it uses length, and is measured in units (one dimension = perimeter). Trace the lid. Show students the lid and ask them to describe it. It has length and width. Hold on to its edge to show that it does have some thickness, but for the purpose of the experiment it is regarded as essentially flat. The lid, then, has two dimensions, length and width. Place centimeter unit cubes to cover the lid. The area (area covered-up) is units squared (two dimensions = area). Then show the container with the lid on it to the class and ask for its description. It has length, width, and depth, which is three dimensions. Place centimeter unit cubes into the container until it is filled and place the lid on top. The volume is the amount inside—count cubes and is units cubed (three dimensions = volume).

Another noteworthy thing in this lesson is to employ a summary for his students. Excellent! We must always review as a closure for our students to help them see the big picture of the day. They leave the class with the sense of the purpose and can use that to connect their old and new knowledge.

Case 8
The Importance of
Sample Size: Posing
High-Level Questions
to Build Understanding
Fifth-Grade Mathematics

CASE SETTING

Danika Fulton taught this lesson at Harry H. Hughes Elementary School in late March from 11:00 to 12:30. This was her fifth year of teaching. Of the ten girls and thirteen boys in the class, 44 percent were African American, 30 percent Asian, 17 percent white, and 9 percent Hispanic. Thirty percent were or had been FARMs. The class was a combination of fourth- and fifth-grade students, but the fourth-graders were in an accelerated program, so all the students were learning fifth-grade math. The room had three computers and a printer along the back wall of the room. Student desks were arranged as long tables, and each table had roughly six students at it. The lesson focus was on sampling.

CASE OVERVIEW

The following excerpt is from a lesson that Ms. Fulton
described as "accelerated for fifth grade" (interview). The
teacher chose the lesson because it fit with their data collection unit and because it reviewed fractions and percentages. The primary goal of the lesson was for the students
to understand how the size of a sample was related to its
accuracy. As this was an accelerated class, it is not surpris-
ing that the Common Core Standard most closely related
to the case appears in the standards for grade 7. Rather
than simply telling the students that a large sample likely
produces more accurate results, Ms. Fulton posed an in-
vestigation to help them understand this fact. She stated
that "the kids are more likely to be able to understand
what's going on when they figured it out as opposed to
you just telling them." The intent of this scenario is to illustrate how Ms. Fulton posed high-level questions to help
her students understand the concept of a sample.

RELATED COMMON CORE STATE STANDARD

Grade 7
Statistics and Probability
Standard 1:

- Understand that statistics can be used to gain information
  about a population by examining a sample of the population;
  generalizations about a population from a sample are valid
  only if the sample is representative of that population; understand that random sampling tends to produce representative
  samples and support valid inferences.

THE CASE

The class began with a quick verbal warm-up in which students identified the factors of numbers. Then, without a pause Ms. Fulton asked, "Who's hungry?" She proceeded to show the students a bag of jellybeans and to describe all the colors in the bag as she wrote the names of the colors on the board. "I have green jellybeans; I have yellow ones; I have black! Who likes black jellybeans? I have pink ones, red ones, orange ones, purple ones, and white ones. I have a question." A student responded with "I knew it!" and the class laughed.

Ms. Fulton continued. "If I wanted to know—let's say my favorite jellybeans are the orange ones—if I wanted to know what percentage of this bag of jellybeans are orange, how would I figure it out?" Rather than allowing the students to respond immediately, she asked them to talk about it for a few minutes with the students at their table. Discussions were brief but lively. After a very short time, Ms. Fulton asked, "All right, what are some ways we can figure it out? How can I figure that out? Paris?" The student explained that she would find the total number of jellybeans and then count how many there were of each color. Ms. Fulton restated the student's response to make sure she understood the student's method and then asked for a different way.

A second student offered a similar approach but suggested that the colors be separated into piles for ease of counting. Ms. Fulton then asked if anyone had a method that did not require counting all the jellybeans, but no one offered one. She continued, "Have you ever heard things, like in the newspaper, they might say one in every four kids experiences bullying at some point. Have you ever heard

of that? Did they ask you?" The class acknowledged that
no one had asked them personally, and Ms. Fulton asked
how the newspaper could make such a claim if it did not
ask everyone. A student suggested that "they probably got
a group of kids, like a group of four or something and they
asked them if they were ever bullied and everyone present
said that."

Ms. Fulton responded, "Okay, so maybe they got a
group. How many did you think? They just got a group
of four?" Students began suggesting larger numbers, ranging from eight to forty-eight. "What is that called?" asked
Ms. Fulton. "What is the word called when you take a
small group to try to make some kind of general statement
about a larger group? Because it's not possible to get to
all the kids in the world to ask them a question. It takes a
lot of time, a lot of work, money; it's not easy to do. What
is it called . . . that group of people they use?" After a
student offered "guinea pigs," Ms. Fulton wrote the word
"sample" on the board, and the students responded by
saying the word aloud.

Ms. Fulton elaborated on the definition of the word
and explained that they were going to use samples to
find the percentage of orange jellybeans in the bag. As
she gave each student five jellybeans, she asked them to
take out their books and turn to the lesson on page 185,
titled "Sampling Candy Colors." The assignment was to
calculate a percentage based on a sample of ten jellybeans
and compare that to the percentage based on a sample of
one hundred jellybeans. Students were to work in pairs to
obtain the smaller sample and work as a class to obtain the

larger sample. Finally, they were asked to count all the jellybeans and compare their samples to each actual number
of jellybeans in the bag.

Ms. Fulton paired the students in a very deliberate
manner, and then paired herself with a student. After
counting how many of each color she and that student
had, Ms. Fulton turned to the class and reminded them
that they had already learned about fractions, decimals,
and percentages and should, therefore, not have any problems computing the percentage of each color. "Hint—that
your percentages should, if you add up all the percentages, what should they total?" The class answered "one
hundred."

Ms. Fulton moved quickly around the room and
checked on the groups. She noticed that a few students were
not computing the percentages correctly and urged them to
make sure they added up to one hundred. Then she gained
the attention of the entire class to illustrate with an example.
"Question for you: Up here, really quickly, please. I need
everyone to stop for a moment. Let's say I have two reds.
Two out of my ten jellybeans are red. How do I find what
percentage that is? Nevue? We want to get a denominator
of what? Of one hundred, that's why it's nice that I gave
you ten. Ten times ten is one hundred. . . . Some of you
are writing two percent [but] that's not gonna work. Check
your percentages; they should equal one hundred when you
add them up."

Altogether, the students had about five minutes to find
the percentage of each color. Then Ms. Fulton handed
each group a piece of paper with an empty circle graph on

it and told them to use the graph to represent their data. After ten minutes, she began posting the graphs on the board and discussing the results. "All right . . . we took a sample from the jellybeans. What is it that I'm really trying to figure out though? What was my initial issue?" A student responded that Ms. Fulton wanted to know the percentage of orange jellybeans in the bag. Ms. Fulton elaborated on the response. "I want to know the percentage of orange. And instead of counting all of the jellybeans in the bag, I want to try to use a sample to figure out the representation." As a class, the students examined the graphs and determined that the amount of orange ranged from 0 percent to 30 percent.

Ms. Fulton asked again why they were using a sample, and a student replied that they wanted "to find out how many orange ones were in the bag." Ms. Fulton pressed for more. "But why a sample? What was a sample going to help us determine?" Nevue said that "you can't ask everybody." The class then discussed the accuracy of the samples and why they might be misleading. Ms. Fulton asked the class what to do about the fact that some of the samples indicated there was no orange in the bag. One student suggested they look at all the samples.

"So let me go back to my question about the one in four kids with the bullying," said Ms. Fulton. "Would I want to use just four kids?" At this point, the students seemed to understand that a larger sample likely would produce a more accurate result. One student said that "if you get a small amount or group you don't know how much it will really be." Ms. Fulton elaborated. "So the larger the sample, the more dependable. So let's see. We have a total of one hundred jellybeans out there. Do you think if we used everybody's jellybeans as the sample it would give us a more accurate count?" The class agreed they should try it. Ms. Fulton added that "right now some of these samples are telling me there are no orange. I know there's some orange out there!"

At this point the class began pooling their samples to create one large sample containing one hundred jellybeans. Ms. Fulton asked each pair how many they had of each color, and she made tallies on the board to account for them. This process took about ten minutes.

After the class finished pooling their data, Ms. Fulton urged them to make sure the colors added up to one hundred and then asked them to determine the percentage of each color in the combined sample. After they calculated the percentage of each color, Ms. Fulton asked another question. "So, how can we figure out how well the sample matched what was actually in the bag in the beginning?" Only one student raised her hand, so Ms. Fulton asked the students to discuss it with a partner. After two minutes, Ms. Fulton asked the question again. A student suggested, "Just look at the—this percent and then look at that percent," indicating they could compare the smaller samples to the sample of one hundred. "No," replied Ms. Fulton, "there is still more in the bag. You only had a sample. Remember, a sample is only a part of it; it isn't the whole thing. Although we used one hundred jellybeans . . . there's still more in the bag." She continued, "We know what the sample is. We know what colors are out there. We need to add what we have left to those."

As a class, they added the remaining jellybeans of each color to the number of jellybeans of each color in the combined sample. After the class found the total number of each color in the bag, Ms. Fulton directed the students to finish answering the questions in the workbook. The workbook asked how well each sample predicted the actual number of jellybeans. It also asked the students to explain whether a larger sample was more trustworthy.

Some students finished the questions and worked on something else while waiting to be dismissed. Others struggled with the last question, and Ms. Fulton assisted them by asking questions. She asked one student, "When they said 0 percent, was that accurate? Was it true?" The student said no but was still uncertain. "Could you give me a hint what I am doing wrong?" asked the student. Ms. Fulton asked another question. "If I wanted to know about candy fifth-graders like, and I'm just going to pick the five people at your table. Would that be okay? Would that then tell me about all kids?" The student said "that's inaccurate" but "it's hard to explain." Ms. Fulton returned to the jellybean task. "There were actually twenty-seven orange jellybeans in the bag. But when we used those little samples, some of them were telling me no [orange jelly-beans]. So, it didn't accurately represent the whole bag. So, think about that concept in your explanation."

After Ms. Fulton okayed everyone's explanation for the last question, she asked the students to look at a graph she made from the sample of one hundred jellybeans. She had used a computer software program to create the graph, and she asked the students to compare it to the graphs they created by hand using their samples of ten jellybeans. She announced that next week they would learn how to use the program to make their own graphs. Then she dismissed the class for lunch.

QUESTIONS

1. In what ways did Ms. Fulton make use of the example about kids that are bullied? How did her use of this real-world context aid her students' understanding of samples?
2. When the students struggled with finding percentages, how did Ms. Fulton respond? How would you have responded?
3. Ms. Fulton often responded to questions with questions. What evidence did you see that the students were accustomed to this practice?
4. In an interview, Ms. Fulton stated her belief that "kids are more likely to be able to understand what's going on when they figured it out as opposed to you just telling them." How does this belief compare to your past experiences with mathematics?

Commentary on Case 8: A Teacher's Perspective

Christine Peterson Tardif

"Who's hungry?" What a great engagement device. I often complain that we talk about food all the time in math, but it really works to focus the students and help them to see real-world situations or to keep their attention. Using the store coupons from the daily newspaper is another real-world example that the students can relate to and is great for getting the students thinking.

When you hear that a student expects questions from a teacher, this shows that questioning is important and done often in this classroom. High-level questioning by teachers helps to move students' thinking in math and to model worthwhile questioning (higher level versus recall) so that students will start to question one another and themselves. The next step is to have the students ask the higher-level questions of one another. The teacher can be a facilitator for some wonderful discourse within the math discussion. Don't feel that you, as the teacher, need to ask every question. Let the students ask one another, even if they disagree or are unsure, let them work it out in groups. They will become more open to risk taking and feel the need to support their thinking with fellow students. Another student won't know the direction of the lesson like the teacher. The teacher may be tempted to ask too many questions and thus move the students in the "proper direction." Why not leave some time for the students to come up with the questions and see where the discussion goes? Discussion with explanation also helps the students when they need to explain in writing for assessments.

Another way to get the students thinking about the concept of "sample" is to use the reference of getting a trial sample of something, for example, when you go to the grocery store and they want you to try a new food, they don't give you the entire box but a small sample to taste. You don't have to eat the whole box to see if you like it. Or if you go to a music store or go online, you can listen to a short sample of the music before you buy the CD or download the song. As teachers we need to know our students and their interests. We need to get into their world to make examples real and interesting to them.

I like to explain percentage to students by writing it out as a fraction and finding the equivalent fraction in one hundredths, then figuring out the percentage: $2/10 = 20/100$ = 20 percent. I have always found that students can write the fraction and say it out loud (and also find the decimal). That seems to help them write the percentage.

Another way to have students explore accurate sample size is to have groups of students do different sample sizes and see who is most accurate. A sample size of ten, then twenty, then fifty or one hundred. The students would see that the closer the sample size comes to the actual size of the data, the more accurate the sample is at predicting the percentages or ratios of items within the data. The teacher used one hundred as a sample of the data. This helps the students with finding the percentage of items within the population. Using the different sample sizes could then be linked to the percentage lesson by finding the percentage of items in the population when the sample size is not one hundred. There are two very important lessons going on here. It would be great to have the percentage lesson and then the sample size lesson and make the connections. This discussion in the math class would help students to solidify their thinking.

Case 9
Continuous versus Discrete Data: Using Concept Attainment to Define Mathematical Terms

Fifth-Grade Mathematics Lesson

CASE SETTING

This lesson was taught by Eddie Wilson at Brookfield Elementary in the afternoon of a day in late spring. Mr. Wilson was in his third year of teaching. The class was an advanced level and lasted one hour. The students were fifth-graders, but the lesson was a sixth-grade lesson. Of his fourteen students, nine were white, two Hispanic, two Asian, and one African American. Five of the students in this advanced class currently or once had an IEP, four were or had been FARMs, and two were currently or had been in ESOL.

For the day's lesson on graphs, students were seated in groups.

CASE OVERVIEW

The following excerpt is from a lesson about graphs. As part of the lesson, Mr. Wilson introduced the students to discrete and continuous data by having the students compare graphs and discuss differences and similarities. The scenario illustrates ways that the teacher helped students understand these terms by building on prior knowledge rather than simply providing a definition. There is no exact match for this content in the Common Core Standards; the closest match is the High School Functions standard that is cited.

RELATED COMMON CORE STATE STANDARD

High School
High School—Interpreting Functions
Standard 5:

- Relate the domain of a function to its graph and, where applicable, to the quantitative relationship it describes. *For example, if the function h(n) gives the number of person-hours it takes to assemble n engines in a factory, then the positive integers would be an appropriate domain for the function.*

THE CASE

The lesson began with a warm-up of review problems from the previous day's lesson. There were eight problems on the warm-up, including substitution, evaluating expressions, order of operations, and the distributive property. The students had eight minutes to complete the problems, and after a discussion of the solutions, Mr. Wilson began a lesson about graphs.

"Okay," began Mr. Wilson. "What is the purpose of a graph?" A student responded, "A graph is to display information so we can read it. It's easier to read it." Mr. Wilson agreed with the student and elaborated. "Graphs are visual displays of data that allow us to make quick interpretations of what is going on."

Mr. Wilson gave the students at each table a worksheet covered in graphs. He directed their attention to the set of four graphs at the top of the page and said, "I want you to figure out what is the same and what is different about those four graphs up there. What do they have in common and what do they have that are different?" He told them they had one minute to discuss the graphs with the students at their tables, and he set his timer.

Mr. Wilson used an overhead projector to display the four graphs during the discussion (see Graph Set I):

After the timer sounded, Mr. Wilson asked what the students noticed was the same about the four graphs. "All the graphs increase," said a girl. Mr. Wilson asked a different student to elaborate on the response. "Okay, how do we know that they increase?" The student stated that the lines were moving upward.

"Upward, upward, upward," replied Mr. Wilson. "Okay. Sam, did your group get anything else that was the same?" Sam had no other similarities to offer, so Mr. Wilson asked the students at the back table what they thought. These students offered something *different* about the graphs, pointing

A.

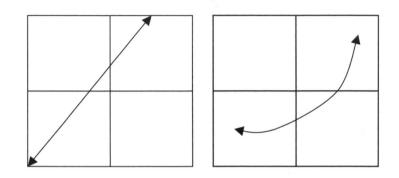

B.

C.

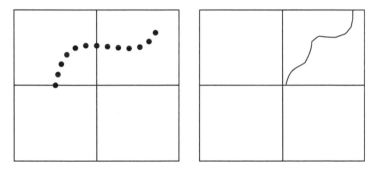

Graph Set I

out that only the first graph "starts from the bottom" and "goes to the top." Mr. Wilson responded with a question. "So how is it that we can make a general, a general difference out of that?" A student offered that the graphs "have different starting points."

Mr. Wilson asked for other differences. A student suggested that only one was a straight line. Another student remarked that "they are not all lines." A third student said that the third graph was the only one that did not increase the whole time. It "sort of stays in the same place for a part of it." Mr. Wilson acknowledged these answers and then asked, "Is this information the same as this information?" He pointed to Graph B and Graph C as he spoke. The students said they were not the same, but one girl remarked that, "None of these are made to be the same." Mr. Wilson altered his question slightly. "Okay. But how, *how* is this information different from this information?"

The students continued to struggle. One student said that the graphs with the dots on it showed differences between things. Mr. Wilson added that the curved line was "continuous" and asked, "What is the first thing that we do when we are plotting a line on a coordinate plane? What is the first thing that we do? After we gather our coordinates and when it's time to actually do the graphing, what is the first thing that we do? Andre?" The boy suggested that the next step would be to plot the points. Mr. Wilson elaborated. "We put the coordinates down, correct? Okay. Could these be the coordinates?" He pointed to Graph C. The students said the dots could be coordinates, but one girl added that "it's not a line yet."

Mr. Wilson emphasized this distinction, saying that when the dots are not connected, "it's telling us something different." He added that the dots were "actual points of data, but they're called discrete pieces of data." He contrasted it with the other three graphs, pointing as he said, "See this, this is continuous. See this, this is continuous. See this, this is continuous." Then he pointed again to the graph with the dots. "This is what we call, and write this above this one, discrete." Then he pointed to the solid curve and said, "And that is data that is going to tell us . . . a completely different story. This is continuous."

Mr. Wilson asked students to examine the next set of four graphs, asking again for similarities and differences. Graph Set II (p. 107) was similar to Graph Set I except the graphs were all decreasing. Instead of one minute, he said he would give them "forty seconds because we've done one. We should be ready to roll with this." During that time, Mr. Wilson observed what the students wrote. When the timer sounded, he stated that "all of these decrease." He then asked for the students to share their observations.

One girl remarked that "they're all basically the same lines, as in graph set I, except for they decrease." Mr. Wilson elaborated. "Oh, so they show the same sort of movement, the same sort of information just in a decreasing mode." Another student said that the last graph was discrete, and Mr. Wilson compared it to the discrete graph in the first set, saying that it would "show the same type of movement." Mr. Wilson also compared some of the other graphs in the two sets, pointing out that the graphs showing straight lines were "constant" whereas others had lines that were "kind of broken."

A.

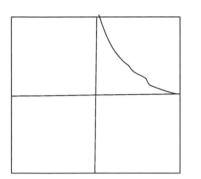

B.

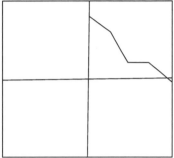

C.

D.

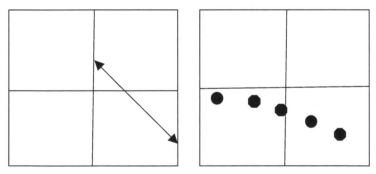

Graph Set II

The class soon moved to differences among the graphs. One student offered that for three of the graphs, "their lines all start on quadrant one." Mr. Wilson acknowledged the response and asked for other differences in Graph Set II. A girl suggested, "They're not all lines." A boy added that only Graph C had a straight line.

"Okay," said Mr. Wilson. "What is graph A here? What type of graph is it?" A boy responded that it was continuous. "What type is graph B?" asked Mr. Wilson. Several students said that it is continuous. Mr. Wilson continued. "Graph C?" Once again, several said it is continuous. "Which makes Graph D . . . ?" Mr. Wilson paused, and several students filled in the silence by saying "discrete."

At this point a boy asked, "Mr. Wilson, how do you know they're continuous?" Mr. Wilson asked the student to repeat his question. "How do you know when a graph is continuous?" asked the boy. Mr. Wilson did not answer. Instead, he asked "Well, can you tell me? Look at which ones we say are continuous and which ones are not continuous. Which ones are discrete?" The student said the continuous graphs were connected. "Connected how?" asked Mr. Wilson. "By a line," replied the student. Mr. Wilson challenged the student. "What happens if I do this? What if I do this?" he asked as he connected a few of the dots. The student said it was still discrete but asked, "They all have to be together?" Mr. Wilson replied, "In order for it to be continuous, it has to be . . ." and then he paused. The student filled in the silence with "together." Mr. Wilson elaborated, stating that it had to be "a constant line."

The last fifteen minutes of the class were spent on a third set of four graphs. The set of graphs plotted distance against time and were accompanied by a set of questions. The focus of the questions was to interpret the information in the graphs, including whether the graphs showed someone speeding up, slowing down, or traveling at a constant rate. At the end of that discussion, Mr. Wilson indicated that tomorrow's lesson would involve solving equations.

QUESTIONS

1. Did Mr. Wilson ever formally define continuous or discrete data? Why not? What would you have done in this situation?
2. Why did Mr. Wilson spend the time to ask students what they noticed about the graphs when he could have just pointed to the fact that some were continuous? What benefit might this kind of questioning have?
3. How did Mr. Wilson's questions change throughout the lesson?

II
PERSPECTIVES
ON TEACHING:
COMMENTARIES

A Matter of Principle: Evidence of Learner-Centered Psychological Practices among Effective Teachers

Patricia A. Alexander

The cases offered in this enlightening volume came from the work of teachers who participated in the High-Quality Teaching Project. When the High-Quality Teaching Project was first conceptualized, researchers contemplated various theoretical frameworks that might serve in the design and implementation of this important undertaking (Valli and Croninger, 2001). Certainly the literature was replete with discussions of exceptional or master teachers and of pedagogical practices deemed to be appropriate for all students or for those identified with special needs, such as children raised in a culture of poverty (Kilpatrick, Swafford, and Findell, 2001). One of the frameworks that proved useful to us, especially in the development of assessment measures, was the Learner-Centered Psychological Principles (LCPs) (American Psychological Association Board of Educational Affairs, 1995; Learning-Centered Principles Work Group of the APA Board of Educational Affairs, 1997). Those principles, which arose from extended discussions among renowned psychological researchers, were founded on more than a century of educational philosophy and empirical research within five broad areas: development and individual differences; the knowledge base; strategic processing or executive functioning; motivation and affect; and situation or context.

For the purpose of this commentary, I return to those five areas of research to consider what lessons about learner-centered psychological principles can be derived from select teaching cases presented in this volume. Specifically, I want to talk about general patterns that I observed across these illustrative cases and use the choices and activities of just one teacher to highlight those patterns: Danika Fulton (Case 8), who provides us insights about teaching mathematics to a diverse class of fourth- and fifth-graders.[1]

My reason for returning to LCPs is to explore the degree to which these principles, derived from theory and research, remain viable when put into the context of the classroom and placed in the hands of a competent teacher like Ms. Fulton who is operating within the challenging and dynamic context that is today's classroom. What as-

---

1 See companion volume, *Upper Elementary Reading Lessons: Case Studies for Real Teaching* for a comparable analysis of reading lessons.

pects of the principles were consistently and more readily apparent in the practices of this highly effective teacher, and which principles were less evident? Further, what explanations can be forwarded for those principles that are strongly espoused in the literature but not often seen in the day-to-day activities of such a select teacher?

DEVELOPMENT AND INDIVIDUAL DIFFERENCES

> Learning, although ultimately a unique adventure for all, progresses through various common stages of development influenced by both inherited and experiential/environmental factors.
>
> —Alexander and Murphy, 1998, p. 36

An intriguing pattern that emerged in this case was the contrast between Ms. Fulton's thoughtful attention to the developmental level of students as a whole, but the more limited consideration of individual student's unique strengths or needs. It was quite evident that Ms. Fulton was aware of and responsive to the overall developmental level of her students. As we look in her classroom, we see a teacher who has chosen mathematics activities that are well matched to the ages, capabilities, life experiences, and overall interests of her students. In addition, Ms. Fulton is vigilant for signs that she has either chosen well or missed her instructional marks, and she is ready to make whatever adjustments seem appropriate. For instance, as Ms. Fulton began her lesson on sampling, she had the sense that her students' understanding of calculating percentage may well be fragile. Thus, she took time to refresh their memories and did so with a task that was very concrete and appealing to these fourth- and fifth-graders.

Unless teachers like Ms. Fulton are attuned to the developmental level of their students, they cannot hope to guide their students toward optimal academic development. However, effective teaching and learning also requires educators to pay attention to students' *unique* cognitive, motivational, sociocultural, and physical attributes; that is, their individual differences. For instance, we can assume that Ms. Fulton used her knowledge of students' mathematical abilities as well as their personality characteristics when she very deliberately created the student pairs for her sampling exercise.

What we do not see, however, is how such knowledge and awareness of students' individual differences translate into the individualization of curricular materials and activities. Generally speaking, Ms. Fulton appears to deal with student diversity through the use of small instructional groups who work on similar or collaborative learning activities. Why would that be the case? Why would a teacher as competent as Ms. Fulton not demonstrate greater sensitivity to students' individual strengths and needs through lesson modifications or personalized tasks? The simplest explanation might be that teachers do not have the time or the freedom to modify instruction to match the uniqueness of an entire class of students. As an alternative, teachers may be able to introduce individual and independent activities for students that are sprinkled into the curriculum.

THE KNOWLEDGE BASE

One's existing knowledge serves as the foundation of all future learning by guiding organization and representations,
by serving as a basis of association with new information,
and by coloring and filtering all new experiences.

—Alexander and Murphy, 1998, p. 28

If there has been one learner-centered psychological principle that has found its way into the routine practices of
competent teachers it relates to the tremendous influence
that students' prior knowledge and experiences exert on
their subsequent learning. Consistently in the current
cases, these effective teachers took care to activate their
students' existing knowledge relative to the topic or skill
under consideration. Often through initial questioning or
through some form of small group activity, the capable
educators represented in these mathematics cases sought
to draw out and build on what their students already understood or on their existing facilities.

As a strategic educator, Ms. Fulton was especially careful to bring her students' existing knowledge and experiences to the foreground when she anticipated that the en-
suing concept or task would be especially abstract, novel,
or challenging. Ms. Fulton observed this tendency when
she started the lesson on sampling by pulling out the jellybeans and posing questions about picking out orange jellybeans from the bag. During this lesson, Ms. Fulton also
used student pairs and small group discussions as mecha-
nisms for eliciting even more background knowledge.

If I have a particular concern with what I discerned in this chosen case, it was that the approaches Ms. Fulton used to activate students' knowledge base occasionally had the appearance of well-practiced techniques or classroom routines. Although such routines are necessary elements within a highly functional classroom (Shulman, 1987), they may have the secondary effect of lessening the depth of reflection in which students engage. Consequently, teachers would be advised to use various knowledge activation techniques and to use them in a flexible manner—just enough novelty or creativity to keep students on their toes.

MOTIVATION AND AFFECT

> Motivational or affective factors, such as intrinsic motivation, attributions for learning, and personal goals, along with the motivational characteristics of learning tasks, play a significant role in the learning process.
>
> —Alexander and Murphy, 1998, p. 33

Young or novice learners require learning environments that pique their interests and energize them. But they also need help to set the seeds for deeper and more durable forms of motivation that will promote their academic development. As these mathematics cases make apparent, highly capable teachers like Ms. Fulton have the ability to establish a caring and motivating learning environment (Mitchell, 1993). Through their choice of activities, interaction styles, and general concern for their students, these teachers have established a learning community that encourages participation. For example, even though Ms.

Fulton did not shy away from correcting students' misunderstandings or directing them toward more conventional meanings or procedures, she did so in a nonjudgmental way.

So, when Ms. Fulton was working with her students on calculating percentages, she moved from group to group encouraging their efforts and gently correcting them when their procedures were inefficient. At one point, she decided that the entire class would benefit from some reteaching of the concept and procedure related to calculating percentages. Yet, throughout the process the students remained on task and engaged.

Although Ms. Fulton was quite proficient in orchestrating engaging and motivating learning environments, she is seemingly less invested in planting the seeds of individual interest in students. This relates to our earlier discussion of individual differences. What would make this classroom even more learner-centered would be evidence that Ms. Fulton was incorporating the particular interests and experiences of each and every student into the activities within the learning community. Allowing for some degree of student choice and self-determination can be one step toward fostering students' individual interests.

We can speculate for a moment on why there was more collective than individual attention to students' motivational as well as cognitive needs in these classrooms. Perhaps the simplest explanations relate to factors of time and organization. That is, it takes a great deal of planning and implementation time to individualize instruction, to say nothing about the information that teachers would require about each student to make that happen.

Further, curricular organization in the form of lessons, activities, and resources is more geared toward whole class or small group instruction, as we observed throughout these mathematics cases. Consequently, it would fall to the teachers to modify existing curricula to address these personal characteristics. For whatever reasons, one-to-one interactions between teacher and student remain rare occurrences.

STRATEGIC PROCESSING AND EXECUTIVE FUNCTIONING

The ability to reflect on and regulate one's thoughts and behaviors is essential to learning and development.

—Alexander and Murphy, 1998, p. 31

What Ms. Fulton demonstrated by many of her actions in this lesson was awareness that students, even those performing at or above grade level, need support and even explicit instruction in how to operate strategically. For that reason, Ms. Fulton reinforced her students' understanding of procedures for determining percentages.

As we witnessed in this case, however, teachers may be more inclined to *mention* the need for strategic behavior than they are to teach students directly and expressly how to engage in strategic learning. Thankfully, there is a resurgence of interest in the teaching of strategic processing that may well translate into more explicit teaching of critical cognitive and metacognitive procedures (Alexander, Graham, and Harris, 1998). Although I applaud this newfound interest in strategic processing and executive functioning, I and others (Afflerbach, Pearson, and Paris, 2008) remain concerned that important distinctions between skills and strategies, which are both essential for development in any academic domain, are being confused and muddled by researchers and practitioners alike. Thus, while the use of strategies (i.e., effortful, reflective, and nonroutine processes) are mentioned in school curricula, it appears that skills (i.e., automatic, habitual processes) are actually the goal.

SITUATION OR CONTEXT

> Learning is as much a socially shared understanding as it is an individually constructed enterprise.
>
> —Alexander and Murphy, 1998, p. 39

Learning never occurs in a vacuum. It is always influenced by the time and place and by the individuals who populate the classroom environment. Throughout these informative mathematics cases, we observed teachers who were very sensitive to the socially shared nature of learning. Whether they were interacting with the entire class or working with small groups of students, Ms. Fulton and the other effective mathematics teachers often took advantage of the social nature of learning. These educators seemed to recognize that they did not have to be the sole sources of information or feedback in their classrooms, and they appreciated that there were alternative perspectives and approaches to learning and performance that needed to be shared. Nonetheless, Ms. Fulton and these other teachers remained the quiet authorities within their classrooms and ensured that their community of learners functioned effectively and efficiently.

Another feature of these cases that pertains to this principle was the manner in which Ms. Fulton thoughtfully constructed activities that made the learning process more concrete and hands-on for their students. Whether it was Ms. Fulton's bag of jellybeans, examples of milkshakes, or geometric shapes, these highly capable teachers understood that abstract concepts or complex procedures would be better grasped and communicated when situated in more familiar settings with more concrete objects and behaviors. Even their simple act of inviting students to participate verbally or physically in the whole class or small group activities was additional evidence that these educators were skilled at harnessing the power of the situation and context to facilitate their students' learning.

If there is a question regarding this particular learner-centered principle, it is the issue of transfer. Although concrete, hands-on, and highly familiar activities are effective tools in the acquisition of concepts and procedures in mathematics, the dependency on such tools should wane over time, as should students' dependency on either human or nonhuman resources in the learning environment. Ideally, the concepts and procedures learned well in one context or situation should, in effect, migrate or transfer to other relevant situations. In this way, students' knowledge, strategies, and skills become broader and deeper and do not remain tentative or context-reliant. For example, we would hope that students in Ms. Fulton's room could eventually understand the concept of sampling and the role of sample size in contexts other than that of jellybeans and bullying.

CONCLUDING THOUGHTS

Throughout this volume, I have had the pleasure of encountering a number of teachers who have dedicated themselves to the academic development of their students. Moreover, these educators have embodied much of the knowledge and processes described in the Learner-Centered Psychological Principles and the vast literature upon which those principles were based. We can be encouraged that there are educators like Ms. Fulton who face the challenges and complexities that are inherent within the educational system with such competence and professionalism. As educational researchers, we benefit from the lessons these educators provide us, just as their students benefit daily.

Moral Perspectives on Teaching Mathematics

Daria Buese

The word "moral" is one that causes uneasy feelings in some people, especially when used in the same sentence with the word "teaching." For these individuals, the idea that teaching is a moral endeavor inspires visions of children being led to a specified belief or value system. Indeed, when we talk about morals we *are* talking about what is valued by society at large, and the thought of teachers addressing moral values in school simply makes some people uncomfortable. One inevitable question— "Whose morals are we talking about?"—nearly always arises when conversations about education turn to the idea that teaching and moral values are intertwined, and it may be the very question that pops into your mind as you read this commentary. Teachers, whether or not they speak about their teaching in moral terms, display moral values (for better or for worse) every day in their work with their students.

In this commentary I examine the moral dimensions of teaching (for better) in the practice of one of the teachers whose lesson is presented in this book. I begin by presenting a short introduction to what I mean by the moral dimensions of teaching and examine ideas of other scholars on the subject. It is my intent in writing this commentary to provide fuel for thought on the moral aspects of your own teaching because the very act of teaching sends moral messages to students in virtually everything teachers do in their classrooms. Teachers can either be cognizant of this condition of their work or deny it, but I steadfastly believe that recognizing it gives us a way to analyze and improve our practice. As moral agents we help make schools into places where children can flourish socially and intellectually. Rather than shying away from conversations about the moral dimensions of our teaching for fear of controversy, such discussions should be encouraged for their potential to advance commonly shared educational values.

MORAL DIMENSIONS

The literature around the moral dimensions of teaching encompasses a wide range of issues, including broad societal concerns about the purposes of schooling. As important and interesting as these issues are, they can also confound discussions about what is moral in teaching practice, so I will not address the larger moral landscape of teachers' work here. Rather, I am more concerned about the moral meaning in the day-to-day work teachers do with their students. Teachers cannot avoid sending moral messages to students, and it is in accepting this fact of school life that they can begin to notice how the way they interact with students and the instructional decisions they make convey moral meaning. David Hansen (2001) portrays this idea eloquently and provocatively by stating that "teaching is a moral endeavor because it influences directly the quality of the present educational moment" (p. 831).

Consider what the present educational moment might entail as you think about the moral dimensions of teaching— I offer a few suggestions. Teachers send moral messages to students through their choices of instructional materials and how they present intellectual ideas (Fenstermacher, Osguthorpe, and Sanger, 2009; Jackson, 1986; Tom, 1984; Valli, 1990). Teachers also model moral values of respect and care through the way they talk to their students and listen to their ideas. When teachers consistently call for similar behavior in their students and when they instill the virtues of learning and teaching that Starratt (2005) identifies as presence (connection to the content being studied), authenticity (truthfulness to self or being "real"), and responsibility (understanding learning as a value and willingly participating in it), they help students recognize and practice behaviors that contribute to learning for all of their students. By getting to know their students, what they like, dislike, the things they care about, their lives outside of school, teachers develop responsive, reciprocal relationships with their students that help students feel cared for (Noddings, 1984). When students feel cared for and cared about, they are more willing to take intellectual risks, which, even when modest, can advance their understanding of academic concepts.

Fenstermacher (2001) helps us understand the moral in teaching by describing what he terms the "manner in teaching." This is a method in which teachers instill moral and intellectual values in students.[1] He explains that manner in teaching is what teachers do to convey virtuous conduct. With attention to the contentiousness of certain words, he reminds us that some people would argue that a teacher's "manner" could include conduct that is good or bad. In his research about the moral manner in teaching he states that his interest is in understanding the manner in teaching that "picks out what is good, moral, sound, and defensible about persons, rather than what is bad, immoral, silly or stupid about them" (p. 649). It is in this vein that I highlight some of the moral dimensions of teaching that appear in this book.

When the researchers (myself included) who collected the data that resulted in this book set out to understand the practices of mathematics teachers, we were more interested in their teaching of content than the moral dimensions of their teaching. However, as I have noted, teaching is imbued with moral meaning, so even in the short excerpts of lessons presented here, we can see how the teachers conveyed virtuous conduct and created learning environments that supported their students' intellectual and moral development. I could easily pick out the moral dimensions of teaching in any of the lessons featured in this book. However, I focus on just one. I do this in an effort to be succinct, but also because moral messages are often subtly sent—they may be conveyed through tone of

---

1 See the *Journal of Curriculum Studies, 33*(6): 2001, for articles produced by the Manner in Teaching Project, directed by Gary Fenstermacher and Virginia Richardson. The articles in this journal provide insight into what is morally salient in teachers' day-to-day work. The authors also investigate the moral grounding of schools and classrooms and provide clear images and discussion of how teachers nurture the moral development of their students.

voice, a look, or a nod. Therefore, I've selected an example that is more overt and in doing so hope to make "moral" and "teaching" more compatible concepts for those who do not (yet) view them as such.

MS. SMITH: CASE 2

The title of Ms. Smith's lesson, "Fractions, Decimals and Percentages: Evoking Student Reasoning" gives an indication of the most obvious moral dimension of teaching in her lesson. The case overview states "the teacher attempts to help students make public links between their use of procedures or operations and the reasons for doing so." It also points out that this practice appears to be done to help not only the student who is answering the question, but also the students who are observing the student's work. As we have seen in both of the preceding examples, teachers convey moral messages by explicating desirable intellectual dispositions, which was precisely the goal of Ms. Smith's lesson.

This lesson was teacher led, even though it shows students presenting their work and doing a good deal of the talking. Ms. Smith's class, like Ms. Hinton's, had students from diverse backgrounds. A third of them were designated as ESOL or had recently exited ESOL status. Ms. Smith gave students ample opportunities to explain their thinking, but she elaborated on their responses to ensure they were hearing the correct terminology and connecting it to the appropriate procedures. This again is an example of a well-executed academic task structure. I include this second example of the practice to illustrate it in a mathematics lesson. Just as Mr. DiLoretto and Ms. Hinton coached their students in discourse that led to the acquisition of literacy,[2] Ms. Smith coached her students in mathematical discourse. She reminded them repeatedly about what high-quality work entails. By consistently prodding them to be explicit about their reasoning, she gained knowledge about their understanding and was able to promote intellectual virtues that support learning.

There is one other aspect of Ms. Smith's teaching that stands out as an example of leading students to or exposing them to valued intellectual dispositions. When the students were working independently at their seats, Ms. Smith noticed that Jacob was struggling with a problem. She patiently and persistently coached Jacob so he could realize the error in his thinking. Another teacher may have simply pointed out his error or shown him how to solve the problem. Through this interaction with Jacob, Ms. Smith demonstrated to him that his learning was important to her, he was worth her time, and that tenacity is a necessary virtue for problem solving.

The relationship between fractions and decimals is a difficult concept for many fourth-graders to grasp. If you think about being a nine-year-old person who hasn't completely made sense of that concept, consider how an instructional manner, as exemplified by Ms. Smith's manner with Jacob, might make the difference between the delay or advancement of the child's mathematical growth. I could tell from her students' responses throughout the scenario that the kind of didactic instruction Ms. Smith demonstrated with Jacob was common to her instruction with all of her students. Maintaining this kind of instruc-

---

2 See companion volume, *Upper Elementary Reading Lessons.*

tion throughout the day can be exhausting (or at times exhilarating) for teachers, but doing so gives students all kinds of moral messages about what it means to do mathematics well. Teachers like Ms. Smith would argue that such effort is well worth the achievement of students' intellectual independence.

MORE FUEL FOR THOUGHT

I had the privilege to observe some of the lessons that were presented in this book and talk to the teachers about their teaching. As you might expect, their attention to the moral dimensions of teaching was much richer in the real life of their classrooms than these lesson excerpts reveal. However, I maintain that my ability to characterize "the moral" in their practices, despite the abbreviated versions of their lessons as they are presented here, confirms how morally saturated the act of teaching is. The example of the moral dimensions of teaching I commented on may seem on the surface to be commonplace. You might conclude that Ms. Smith was simply teaching in ways that are reasonably expected or that moral virtues related to intellectual growth are a natural result of teaching certain content. You may wonder, "Did the teachers in this book really think about their practice in moral ways?" I assert, with certainty, that these teachers did approach the moral dimensions of their practice on a conscious level to promote highly valued intellectual and behavioral traits. They constructed their lessons in ways that disposed students to habits of mind that contributed to their intellectual development. They created classroom atmospheres in which students received respect from others and learned the value of returning it. And, they developed caring relationships with their students in ways that helped students realize that positive behaviors and attitudes reap greater rewards than negative ones. The moral values these teachers expressed appeared purposefully, not unconsciously, within the "present educational moments" of their lessons because they understood and accepted that moral agency is implicit in the practice of teaching.

Mathematics Lessons: Perspective from the Special Education Math Literature

Paula Maccini

Ms. Evelyn Keller, a teacher with thirty-four years of experience, taught her seven fifth-grade students with special needs multiplication and problem-solving skills, as reflected in Cases 1 and 4. Further, Mr. Eddie Wilson, a teacher of three years, taught an advanced lesson on graphs to fifth-grade students (Case 9). The cases incorporated effective instructional practices and principles that promote accessibility within the math curriculum for all learners. These practices and principles will be discussed below relative to characteristics of students with special needs in math, as well as examples from the scenarios. Suggestions for future practice will be also delineated based on the literature.

Students with special needs, particularly learning disabilities (LD), experience a variety of difficulties that impede their math performance. Specifically, more than 60 percent of students with LD have significant problems in math (Light and DeFries, 1995). These include problems with basic mathematics (e.g., facts, symbol identification, and computation), as well as higher level mathematics and problem solving skills (e.g., algebra, geometry). Further, many students with LD have memory deficits and experience problems with retaining information (e.g., multistep problems, procedural strategies) over time and generalizing to other tasks (Hudson and Miller, 2006). According to these authors, the use of explicit teaching principles and procedural strategies has been shown to help students with difficulties in math. Explicit teaching principles include providing (1) an advance organizer (i.e., reviewing of prerequisite skills, stating the objective and relevance); (2) demonstration (i.e., thinking aloud while modeling the task, involving students, and monitoring understanding); (3) guided practice (i.e., providing support and slowly fading teacher assistance as students become more independent); (4) independent practice (i.e., students work on the problem independently); and (5) maintenance (i.e., providing cumulative practice over time). Procedural strategies refer to sequenced steps that lead to problem solution and are used to help students remember information (Hudson and Miller, 2006).

To further promote accessibility for all learners within the curriculum, the Center for Applied Special Technology (CAST, 2010) identified three overarching principles of Universal Design for Learning (UDL) for curricular decision making. The three principles include: (1) providing options for representing information to promote student comprehension and perception (e.g., color contrasts on screens, speech to text programs, graphic displays, and virtual manipulatives); (2) providing options for action and expression/communication (e.g., adaptive keyboards, manipulatives, goal-setting strategies); and (3) providing options for engagement to promote and retain student interest (e.g., reducing possible distractions, providing authentic problem situations, self-regulation and self-reflection strategies).

The three cases incorporated a number of explicit instructional practices and general UDL principles. For instance, in terms of explicit instructional practices, Mr. Wilson incorporated the use of an advance organizer, demonstration, and guided practice within the lesson. The teacher provided an advance organizer by considering students' prior background knowledge and prerequisite skills for the target lesson (i.e., included a warm-up of previously learned skills, reviewed the purpose of a graph). During the demonstration, Mr. Wilson involved students by generating a class discussion at the beginning of the lesson to increase student interest and to encourage critical thinking ("I want you to figure out what is the same and what is different about those four graphs up there"). Students were encouraged to describe the critical features of the four graphs in terms of similarities and differences and were asked to elaborate on their responses ("Okay, how do we know that they increase?").

Mr. Wilson also monitored student understanding ("how is this information different from this information") and prompted students to consider related prior knowledge to help them with the concept attainment ("What is the first thing we do when we are plotting a line on a coordinate graph?). He also guided student understanding of discrete and continuous data by prompting students to think of distinctions across the second set of graphs, followed by a third set of graphs that related to interpreting graphed data. The lesson reflected general UDL principles, including providing options for representation, expression, and engagement by incorporating graphic displays of information, establishing a community of discourse as students shared key characteristics, and varying the level of teacher support by scaffolding the prompts provided. Although Mr. Wilson incorporated the noted UDL principles and explicit teaching practices, it would also be helpful for students to address the relevance of the target skills and how the information relates to the real world to enhance generalization. Further, the students can explore the concepts using alternate modes of representation with the use of technology, including graphing calculators or talking graphing calculators to further enhance student exploration and accessibility.

In the remaining two cases, Ms. Keller illustrated the use of (1) guided practice and teacher prompts to encourage students to think of a new approach to solving a word problem; and (2) illustrated how to divide a task into manageable parts to support student understanding. First, through teacher prompting, students were encouraged to think of a more efficient method for solving word problems (using multiplication rather than repeated addition). Ms. Keller's actions exemplified the UDL principles of providing options for engagement and representation by discussing relevant information in the word problem and encouraging students to share their approach to solving the problem prior to thinking of an alternative method ("Anyone got a shortcut?"). Ms. Keller could have also included visual cues (e.g., highlight, circle, underline) to help students with LD identify and remember the relevant features to the word problem, as well as a conversion chart to help students remember and transfer the information. Further, in addition to drawing pictures, Ms. Keller could have incorporated the use of manipulatives or virtual manipulatives as additional options for representation to promote flexibility in representation. For instance, using a concrete-representational-abstract (CRA) instructional sequence has been shown to help students with LD understand math concepts and transition to more abstract concepts (Hudson and Miller, 2006). Ms. Keller could have included manipulatives to help students represent the concepts (concrete) or virtual manipulatives of the concepts (representational), in addition to number and symbol notation (abstract).

In Case 4, Ms. Keller helped to make a multistep word problem more manageable for students with special needs by dividing the task into substeps. First, Ms. Keller modeled how to identify relevant information by thinking aloud ("First, determine what . . . we know"). She then prompted students through redirection (i.e., she asked students to reread the word problem for information, refocus their attention on the current word problem, and to elaborate on an answer). Ms. Keller could have also provided additional options for representation for both memory and transfer by introducing a procedural strategy to help students with LD remember the steps and corresponding substeps for solving word problems. For example, some procedural strategies include a mnemonic device to help student recall the problem-solving steps, such as the first letter mnemonic, STAR: *S*earch the word problem; *T*ranslate the words into an equation in picture form or represent a picture using manipulatives; *A*nswer the problem; and *R*eview the solution (Maccini and Hughes, 2000; Maccini and Ruhl, 2000).

As noted, the three scenarios incorporated practices including the use of explicit teaching principles, procedural strategies, and UDL principles that have been shown to help students with special needs access the general education mathematics curriculum. Suggestions for future instruction were also delineated based on the needs of students with special needs and the literature.

A Principal's Perspective

Kathy Lynn Brake

As the principal of one of the schools highlighted in this rcsearch study, I was asked to reflect on what I felt makes the difference in developing a school community that exhibits and supports the kind of high-quality teaching seen in these lesson cases. Having been the principal of that school for fifteen years, I would be remiss if I did not describe our school. At the time of the study and ever since "adequate yearly progress" has been measured, our students have met the standards set by the state for each subgroup identified in No Child Left Behind (NCLB). Additionally, at the time of the study, the school had 55 percent of the student population receiving subsidized lunch and was also diverse, with the following demographic breakdown: 19.9 percent African American, 0.3 percent Native American, 12.6 percent Asian, 44.9 percent Hispanic, 22.3 percent white, 13.1 percent special education, 33.1 percent ELL (English language learners). The children are served in a prekindergarten through fifth-grade setting using the home-school model of special education full inclusion. The school also had a Head Start class for three-year-olds. So how does a school support high-quality teaching and what can a principal do to create and sustain that supportive climate?

PERSONAL RELATIONSHIP
BUILDING AND HIGH EXPECTATIONS

Personal relationship building is important in order for children to feel supported during classroom instruction. The teacher cannot expect a child to feel confident in taking risks during the instructional period if that child does not feel safe in responding to questions posed. Children who feel that the environment in which they learn is free from criticism will often open and stretch their minds to new heights of learning. These same children need to be provided with scaffolding questions to lead them to successful responses. It is when this kind of climate has been established and emanates throughout the instructional day that children will have the confidence and encouragement to grow and learn.

Teachers are great enablers—they want and need for children to be successful, sometimes to the extent that they require different responses from different children. Teachers who are enablers often may not continue to challenge and stretch a child; they may ask lower-level questions, accept minimal responses, and when they do this they are not requiring the same learning from all children. Indeed, they are not using high-quality teaching skills. If we are going to narrow, no—if we are going to eliminate—the achievement gap, all staff must have high expectations for all children and must require all children to meet all instructional goals. In order to do this, some of our children will have to have instructional interventions provided to them that include scaffolding of instruction as well as previewing of skills to be learned, and that's what high-quality teachers do. They carefully monitor the learning of these children so that they can intervene appropriately in order for them to be successful on formative and summative assessments.

It is not only important for teachers to have personal relationships with students in their care, but it is equally important for administrators to exhibit these same skills with their staff. A stable, warm, inviting team-building climate must be a part of every school in order for staff and students to meet the high expectations required. You can often feel this kind of climate upon entering a building. You can most certainly detect when it does not exist. Teachers who work in schools that exhibit a warm, inviting, collegial climate are more positive, have high energy, and become so interconnected with one another and the community that they never want to leave. This kind of stable, caring staff works beyond what is required to collaborate and seek just the right strategy to meet the needs of each learner. Every child is owned by every staff member in the building. Every child's success is the direct result of this ownership.

According to Blankstein (2004), "The future of leadership must be embedded in the hearts and minds of the many, and not rest on the shoulders of a heroic few" (p. 210). In order to sustain quality leadership in any school system, systems thinking must be applied to all initiatives. It is through this sense of teaming where principals

learn from other principals through support groups that
sustainability can occur. It is through this sense of teaming where teachers learn from one another and become a
support to one another that sustainability can occur. In
The Fifth Discipline, Peter Senge (2006) wrote, "Tackling
a difficult problem is often a matter of seeing where the
high leverage lies, a change which—with a minimum of
effort—would lead to lasting significant improvement"
(p. 64). Perhaps the leverage point described by Senge is
the professional learning community that is built within
an individual school or within an individual grade level
that focuses on discussing instructional implications after
analyzing common formative assessments.

Peterson and Deal (2002) believe a school's culture
has a powerful impact on what occurs daily in that school.
"A school's culture sharpens the focus of daily behavior
and increases attention to what is important and valued"
(p. 10). Whatever is valued in a school's culture will be
what is practiced within that school. If student achievement is an active ingredient of school culture, then staff
will work collectively in that regard. It becomes the commitment by which the school lives. Productivity on the
part of teachers and students increases when driven by
positive school culture. If data collection, analysis, and
interpretation are important to the members of a school
community, they become a part of its culture. If teachers feel comfortable collaborating to determine needs
for improvement in instruction and in reviewing data on
a regular basis, then collaboration becomes a part of its
culture. The culture of a school is and ought to be shaped
by its leadership.

Principals and teachers must be willing to critically review the data, openly discuss the results found, and determine next steps in instruction. Teachers must learn to work closely together as a team to identify learning outcomes, determine what proficiency looks like, and then monitor the data they gather. They must learn to interact personally and daily with the data they gather. Principals must and should meet on a regular basis with school teams to discuss data and guide teachers in determining instructional implications. Principals must call upon specialists in their schools to help them guide these data discussions. A staff development teacher and reading specialist team working in concert with an administrator can be a valuable part of the grade-level data team discussions. The principal's presence is critical as teachers will increase their acceptance of the data through the supportive discussions about data. Conversations such as these will not be seen as a threat to their professional abilities, but rather as a support in helping the teachers increase student achievement. Every teacher upon entering the profession enters it because he or she wants to help children learn and grow.

MONITORING

The lifeblood of school improvement is student achievement data.

—Rettig et al., 2003, p. 73

Whether mandated by a federal law or imposed by taxpayers who require school systems to be more accountable, the regular and timely analysis of data should be an integral part of every instructional day. "Timely feedback provided throughout a learning experience is referred to as 'formative' assessment as opposed to 'summative' assessment that occurs at the end of a learning experience" (Marzano, 2003, p. 37). Not only should principals and teachers analyze summative data to understand adequate yearly progress, they should also analyze formative data points in order to determine instructional implications and make adjustments to instruction in order to intervene early enough to improve the results of summative data.

School principals play an active role in analyzing and interpreting data in order to meet requirements made by their school systems and the federal government. Yet classroom teachers make the final determination as to what is actually taught on a daily basis. Therefore, it is critical for classroom teachers to increase their skills and abilities in data analysis and interpretation. Educational researchers have concluded that a teacher's use of formative assessments could improve the achievement of students (Marzano, 2003).

Teachers, schools, states, the entire nation are struggling to close or eliminate the achievement gap for students. "While formative assessments can help all pupils, it yields particularly good results with low achievers by concentrating on specific problems of their work and giving them a clear understanding of what is wrong and how to put it right" (Black and Wiliam, 1998, p. 6). Many teachers struggle to improve their instructional practices in an effort to achieve improved educational results with all of their children. If formative assessment is one way to close the achievement gap, then the careful, complete analysis and interpretation of formative assessment results should be an ongoing part of professional growth for every teacher.

In this age of accountability, good teaching will be determined by looking at results (Jerald, 2003). Teachers need to look at the results of their students' formative assessments and be able to analyze them correctly in order to adapt their own instructional practices and make instructional changes related to their analysis. Rettig, Mc-Cullough, Santos, and Watson (2003) determined that teachers should work in teams to design and administer common assessments. It is through this collaborative effort that they analyze results, and student progress becomes a schoolwide concern (Rettig et al., 2003). We are fortunate to have a districtwide curriculum that includes such common assessments. It is imperative that staff are required to work collaboratively to analyze results and determine instructional implications.

Testing and assessment should be integral parts of the educational experience. If schools focus on the high-stakes testing required by the federal government instead of focusing on the instructional practices and formative assessments within the classrooms, they may only get short-term results. Although the collection of data is important to the educational process, it is the careful analysis and interpretation of those data that will change instruction. "While data analysis is the process of counting and comparing, interpreting is making sense of what the analysis tells us" (Killion, 2003, p. 21). It is through this frequent analysis and interpretation of data that teachers will make the decisions that will benefit daily instruction. Therefore, focusing on teachers' instructional decision making after they have given formative assessments will ultimately have greater effects on student achievement and success.

STAFF DEVELOPMENT

Monitoring of data should help the school principal determine if individual classes or grade levels are meeting the school system's benchmarks, thus allowing specialized staff to intervene on an "as needed" basis to assist individual students or teachers. Formative assessment data are used while conferencing with and observing the progress of teachers. The focus of our school system is on internal, consistent staff development. All schools at every level (elementary, middle, and high) have full-time staff development teachers. All elementary schools have reading specialists. Many elementary schools have part-time math content coaches. These support specialists are a critical part of the achievement of students. It is through their conscious commitment to data review that they guide the staff development needs of the teachers in their school. Data are also used to support training needs after careful review from the reading specialist, math content coach, and staff development teacher. Principals may also use the results of these data to project success on state and system summative assessments. Also, administrators, grade-level teams, and support specialists may use these data to guide discussions about curriculum development and implementation, as well as determine the need for academic interventions for individual students. Knowledge of assessments and the ability to analyze and interpret them ought to be an important part of the principal's role as an instructional leader.

As teachers collaborate to identify strengths and weaknesses of instruction through data analysis, they may grow in their ability to refine instruction and teaching strategies to have a greater impact on the academic achievement of students. Schmoker (2003) concluded that classroom teachers can learn to analyze data and, that by doing so, this analysis will have an impact on teaching and achievement. It is through careful analysis and interpretation of formative assessment data that instruction can change to allow students to achieve academic targets. Teams of teachers can learn to work together to analyze data relevant to them and the immediate instruction of their students. Often teachers are presented with summative data that make little sense to them in their daily decision making about instruction. These summative data are often presented at year's end or even at the beginning of the following year, when they cannot impact student instruction as needed in real time.

According to Schmoker (2003), "the primary purpose of analyzing data is improving instruction to achieve greater student success" (p. 23). If analyzing data is critical to students' academic achievement, then those data should be formative data rather than summative, and teachers must be thoroughly trained in analyzing the data to inform instruction. Black and Wiliam (1998) conclude that assessments must be used to adjust teaching and learning in order for them to have a significant impact. The authors state: "For assessment to function formatively, the results have to be used to adjust teaching and learning; thus a significant aspect of any program will be the ways in which teachers make these adjustments" (p. 3).

PROFESSIONAL LEARNING COMMUNITIES

A professional learning community, as defined by DuFour (2003), is one in which "the people have a clear sense of the mission they are to accomplish and a shared vision of the conditions they must create to achieve their mission" (p. 15). He further believes that the entire school system must

> engage teams in a cycle of continuous improvement—gathering and analyzing data and information, identifying weaknesses and areas of concern, working together to develop strategies to address specific weaknesses and concerns, supporting each other as they implement those strategies, gathering new data and information to assess the impact of the strategies and then starting the process all over again. (p. 15)

It is the expectation of our school system that schools and teacher teams will work as a professional learning community.

A strong effort was made in the school district to rewrite our reading and mathematics curriculums to focus on supporting special populations through the scaffolding of instruction to meet the needs of special education students and English language learners. But, in addition, the school system also has an expectation that all teachers will teach all children accelerated indicators. This new curriculum also connects system targets and instructional indicators to the recommended state curriculum. During common planning time teacher teams look closely at the indicators they are teaching to decide how they will monitor success, what multiple measures they will use to determine if a child has met proficiency, and to discuss instructional implications and changes when their instruction has not been successful. It is taking on this responsibility for what a child learns that is also a sign of high-quality teaching.

Feedback to students is a critical part of this practice. "Teachers must possess and be ready to apply knowledge of sound classroom assessment practices" (Stiggins, 2004, p. 26). The feedback a teacher gives on formative assessments is a critical part of a child's individual improvement. Black et al. (2004) state that "feedback that focuses on what needs to be done can encourage all to believe that they can improve" (p. 18). This kind of feedback enhances learning and supports the child to put forth the effort to achieve. By providing this kind of specific feedback educators are "building learning environments that help all students believe that they can succeed at hitting the target if they keep trying" (Stiggins, 2004, p. 24).

In an effort to meet the ever-demanding accountability requirements thrust upon teachers, principals, and school systems by parents, the broader community and the federal and state governments, one must focus on what occurs within the classroom setting as it directly impacts the instructional decisions being made by an individual classroom teacher. One must look at the use of formative assessments to guide instructional decision-making practices. Teachers need to look at assessment as a way to receive feedback about their students' learning so that they can adjust instruction and reteach concepts and skills students have not mastered. Working collaboratively in teacher teams and discussing common formative assessment results is an important staff development practice. The degree of difference in a teacher's ability to analyze and interpret formative assessment data should make a difference in determining instructional implications and increasing student achievement.

PROFESSIONAL GROWTH SYSTEMS

Three professional growth systems have been developed and implemented by our school district: a teacher professional growth system, an administrator professional growth system, and a supporting services professional growth system. Leaders from all the employees' representative organizations played an important role in shaping each professional growth system and each is important in supporting high-quality teaching. This was accomplished through much collaborative effort on the part of the executive staff of the school system. It was an attempt on the part of the school system to improve development, training, retention, and evaluation of all staff.

As a part of the teacher and administrator professional growth systems, consulting teachers and consulting principals were assigned to novice employees and those not performing to standard. These consulting teachers and principals observed their clients and provided regular feedback to them on their practices. They were available to assist their clients in every way possible to ensure their professional success. They were also there to assist in confirming the practices of an underperforming client.

DATA, DATA, DATA

Educators know that the regular use of data analysis has its benefits in improving instruction. In fact, every competent, efficient organization agrees that data are imperative to the growth and success of any business or organization. Seldom does a day go by that data are not reviewed, analyzed, and interpreted for the benefit of the organization. In this age of accountability and with the large amounts of federal, state, and local monies being allocated for educational resources, the American public, elected officials, and local school systems demand an educational payback on their funding. In an effort to hold teachers and school systems accountable for the academic achievement of every child, data gathering and reporting are critical. Yearly summative assessments are only a small fraction of the accountability of student achievement. In order to meet the summative goal, school systems are moving to common formative assessments, monitoring and data gathering of learning indicators, and benchmarking academic growth in reading and mathematics on a regular basis as the school year progresses. To deal adequately with data:

- Teachers must learn to interact personally and daily with data they collect;
- Principals must meet on a regular basis with school teams to discuss data and guide teachers in determining instructional implications;
- Principals must call upon school specialists to help guide these data discussions; and
- During any staff development training, data discussions with teachers must always focus on instructional implications.

PARTNERSHIPS

Our school system has created several important partnerships with universities in an effort to meet the career advancement needs of our support staff as well as to increase the quality of teacher level candidates. One such partnership was initially developed in an attempt to increase the number of minority and male teachers in the school system. Candidates with bachelor degrees were invited to apply to the masters in education program and during this two-year, degree-seeking period they are employed as paraeducators in the schools. As a school that has had many of these program interns for several years, I can attest to its success. From the first day on the job every intern in my school was encouraged to join the professional staff for all staff meetings and preservice trainings. They were plunged into the culture and climate of the school and after the two-year program often remained at the school in teacher level positions. I was able to increase the number of male teachers, African American teachers, and Hispanic teachers through this program. Similar partnerships have been created with another university to increase the number of teacher candidates with special education degrees.

CONCLUSION

One might disagree with how individual states have interpreted and implemented NCLB, but every educator knows that this federal law has caused each of us to look more closely at the performance of subgroups. This has forced us to attack and, yes, with clear, high expectations, attempt to eliminate the achievement gap. Every educator with a conscience and a heart must certainly believe that no matter a child's ethnicity, no matter a child's poverty level, no matter the special needs or second language needs, every child must be encouraged and supported to perform at high academic levels. It is only when we do this that we will finally provide an equal educational opportunity for all children.

References

Afflerbach, P. A., Pearson, P. D., and Paris, S. G. (2008). Clarifying differences between reading skills and reading strategies. *The Reading Teacher, 61*(5), 364–73.

Alexander, P. A., Graham, S., and Harris, K. (1998). A perspective on strategy research: Progress and prospects. *Educational Psychology Review, 10*(special issue), 129–54.

Alexander, P. A., and Murphy, P. K. (1998). The research base for APA's learner-centered psychological principles. In N. M. Lambert and B. L. McCombs (Eds.), *Issues in school reform: A sampler of psychological perspectives on learner-centered schools* (pp. 25–60). Washington, DC: American Psychological Association.

American Psychological Association Board of Educational Affairs. (1995, December). Learner-centered psychological principles: A framework for school redesign and reform. Washington, DC: American Psychological Association. (http://www.apa.org/ed/lcp.html)

Ascher, M. (1991). *Ethnomathematics: A multicultural view of mathematical ideas.* Belmont, CA: Wadsworth.

Ausubel, D. P. (1960). The use of advance organizers in the learning and retention of meaningful verbal material. *Journal of Educational Psychology, 51,* 267–72.

Barnett-Clarke, C. (2001). Case design and use: Opportunities and limitations. *Research in Science Education, 31*(2), 309–12.

Black, P., Harrison, C., Lee, C., Marshall, B., and Wiliam, D. (2004). Working inside the black box: Assessment for learning in the classroom. *Phi Delta Kappan, 86*(1), 9–21.

Black, P., and Wiliam, D. (1998). Inside the black box: Raising standards through classroom assessment. *Phi Delta Kappan, 80*(2), 139–48.

Blankstein, A. M. (2004). *Failure is not an option.* Thousand Oaks, CA: Corwin Press.

Bloom, B. S. (1956). *Taxonomy of educational objectives, handbook I; Cognitive domain.* New York: David McKay.

Borasi, R. (1994). Capitalizing on errors as "Springboards for Inquiry": A teaching experiment. *Journal for Research in Mathematics Education, 25*(2), 166–208.

Bransford, J. D., Brown, A. L., and Cocking, R. R. (Eds.) (1999). *How people learn: Brain, mind, experience, and school.* Washington, DC: National Academy of Science.

Brophy, J. (2004). *Motivating students to learn.* 2nd ed. Mahwah, NJ: Erlbaum.

Carter, K. (1999). What is a case? What is not a case? In M. A. Lundeberg, B. Levin, and H. Harrington (Eds.), *Who learns what from cases and how? The research base for teaching and learning with cases* (pp. 165–75). Mahwah, NJ: Erlbaum.

Center for Applied Special Technology (CAST). (2010). *UDL examples and resources*—Version 1.0. Wakefield, MA: Author.

Chambliss, M., and Graeber, A. (2003, April). Does subject matter *matter?* Paper presented at the meeting of the American Educational Research Association, Chicago.

Common Core State Standards Initiative. Retrieved December 5, 2010, from http://www.corestandards.org/.

DuFour, R. (2003). Building a professional learning community. *The School Administrator, 60*(5), 13–18.

Fenstermacher, G. D. (2001). On the concept of manner and its visibility in teaching practice. *Journal of Curriculum Studies, 33*(6), 639–53.

Fenstermacher, G. D., Osguthorpe, R. D., and Sanger, M. N. (2009). Teaching morally and teaching morality. *Teacher Education Quarterly,* *36*(3), 7–19.

Good, T., and Brophy, J. (2007). *Looking in classrooms.* 10th ed. Boston: Allyn & Bacon.

Grossman, P. (2005). Research on pedagogical approaches in teacher education. In M. Cochran-Smith and K. M. Zeichner (Eds.), *Studying teacher education: A report of the AERA panel on research and teacher education* (pp. 425–76). Mahway, NJ: Erlbaum.

Grossman, P., Schoenfeld, A., and Lee, C. (2005). Teaching subject matter. In L. Darling-Hammond and J. Bransford (Eds.), *Preparing teachers for a changing world: What teachers should learn and be able to do* (pp. 201–31). San Francisco: Jossey-Bass.

Hansen, D. T. (2001). Teaching as a moral activity. In V. Richardson (Ed.), *Handbook of research on teaching* (pp. 826–57). Washington, DC: American Educational Research Association.

Hatano, G. (1982). Learning to add and subtract: A Japanese perspective. In T. P. Carpenter, J. M. Moser, and T. A. Romberg (Eds.), *Addition and subtraction: A cognitive perspective* (pp. 211–23). Hillsdale, NJ: Erlbaum.

Hiebert, J. (2003). What research says about the NCTM standards. In J. Kilpatrick, W. G. Martin, and D. Schifter (Eds.), *A research companion to principles and standards for school mathematics* (pp. 5–24). Reston, VA: National Council of Teachers of Mathematics.

Hudson, P., and Miller, S. P. (2006). *Designing and implementing mathematics instruction for students with diverse learning needs.* Boston: Pearson.

Jackson, P. W. (1986). *The practice of teaching.* New York: Teachers College Press.

Jerald, C. (2003). Beyond the rock and the hard place. *Educational Leadership, 61*(3), 12–16.

Killion, J. (2003). 8 smooth steps. *Journal of the National Staff Development Council, 24*(4), 14–21.

Kilpatrick, J., Swafford, J., and Findell, B. (Eds.). (2001). *Adding it up: Helping children learn mathematics.* Washington, DC: National

Academy Press and the National Reading Council, Mathematics Learning Study Committee, Center for Education, Division of Behavioral and Social Sciences and Education.

Kilpatrick, J., Martin, W. G., and Schifter, D. (Eds.). (2003). *A research companion to Principles and Standards for School Mathematics.* Reston, VA: National Council of Teachers of Mathematics.

Lan, R., and Oxford, R. L. (2003). Language learning strategy profiles of elementary school students in Taiwan. *International Review of Applied Linguistics and Language Teaching, 41*(4), 339–79.

Learner-Centered Principles Work Group of the APA Board of Educational Affairs. (1997, November). Learner-centered psychological principles: a framework for school reform and redesign. Washington, DC: American Psychological Association.

Levin, B. (1999). The role of discussion in case pedagogy: Who learns what? And how? In M. A. Lundeberg, B. Levin, and H. Harrington (Eds.), *Who learns what from cases and how? The research base for teaching and learning with cases* (pp. 139–57). Mahwah, NJ: Erlbaum.

Light, J. G., and DeFries, J. C. (1995). Comorbidity of reading and mathematics disabilities: Genetic and environmental etiologies. *Journal of Learning Disabilities, 28*, 96–106.

Lundeberg, M. A., and Scheurman, G. (1997). Looking twice means seeing more: Developing pedagogical knowledge through case analysis. *Teaching and Teacher Education, 13*(8), 783–97.

Maccini, P., and Hughes, C. A. (2000). Effects of a problem-solving strategy on the introductory algebra performance of secondary students with learning disabilities. *Learning Disabilities Research & Practice, 15*(1), 10–21.

Maccini, P., and Ruhl, K. L. (2000). Effects of graduated instructional sequence on the algebraic subtraction of integers by secondary students with disabilities. *Education and Treatment of Children, 23*(4), 465–89.

Marzano, R. J. (2003). *What works in schools: Translating research into action.* Alexandria, VA: Association for Supervision and Curriculum Development.

Matsumoto, D. (2001). *The handbook of cross-cultural psychology.* New York: Oxford University Press.

Mayer, R. (2002). *The promise of educational psychology*. Upper Saddle River, NJ: Pearson Education.

Mayer, R. (2003). *Learning and instruction*. Upper Saddle River, NJ: Pearson Education.

Merseth, K. (1996). Cases and case methods in teacher education. In J. Sikula, T. Buttery, and E. Guyton (Eds.), *Handbook of research on teacher education* (2nd ed., pp. 722–44). New York: Macmillan.

Mitchell, M. (1993). Situational interest: Its multifaceted structure in the secondary school mathematics classroom. *Journal of Educational Psychology, 85,* 424–36.

National Council of Teachers of Mathematics (NCTM). (1989). *Curriculum and evaluation standards for school mathematics*. Reston, VA: Author.

National Council of Teachers of Mathematics (NCTM). (2000*). Principles and standards for school mathematics.* Reston, VA: Author.

National Council of Teachers of Mathematics (NCTM). (2003*). Research companion to the principles and standards for school mathematics.* Reston, VA: Author.

National Research Council (NRC). (2001). *Adding it up: Helping children learn mathematics*. J. Kilpatrick, J. Swafford, and B. Findell (Eds.). Mathematics Learning Study Committee, Center for Education, Division of Behavioral and Social Sciences and Education. Washington, DC: National Academy Press.

National Research Council (NCR). (2005). *How students learn: Mathematics in the classroom*. Washington, DC: National Academy of Sciences.

Noddings, N. (1984). *Caring: A feminine approach to ethics and moral education*. Berkeley, CA: University of California Press.

Oxford, R. L. (1990). *Language learning strategies: What every teacher should know*. Boston: Heinle/Thomson Learning.

Oxford, R. L. (1996). *Language learning strategies around the world: Crosscultural perspectives*. Manoa: University of Hawaii Press.

Palinscar, A., and Brown, A. (1984). Reciprocal teaching of comprehension-fostering and comprehension-monitoring activities. *Cognition and Instruction, 1*(2), 117–75.

Peterson, K. D., and Deal, T. E. (2002). *The shaping school culture fieldbook*. San Francisco: Jossey-Bass.

Rettig, M. D., McCullough, L. L., Santos, K., and Watson, C. (2003). A blueprint for increasing student achievement. *Educational Leadership*, *61*(3), 71–76.

Rowe, M. B. (1986). Wait time: Slowing down may be a way of speeding up! *Journal of Teacher Education, 37*, 43–50.

Schmoker, M. (2003). First things first: Demystifying data analysis. *Educational Leadership, 60*(5), 22–24.

Senge, R. (2006). *The fifth discipline: The art and practice of the learning organization.* New York: Doubleday/Random House.

Shulman, J. (1992). Introduction. In J. Shulman (Ed.), *Case methods in teacher education* (pp. xiii–xvii). New York: Teachers College Press.

Shulman, L. (1987). Knowledge and teaching: Foundations of the new reform. *Harvard Educational Review, 57*(1), 1–22.

Shulman, L. (1992). Toward a pedagogy of cases. In J. Shulman (Ed.), *Case methods in teacher education* (pp. 1–33). New York: Teachers College Press.

Shulman, L. (2004). Just in case: reflections on learning from experience. In S. Wilson (Ed.), *The wisdom of practice: Essays on teaching, learning, and learning to teach* (pp. 463–82). San Francisco: Jossey-Bass.

Starratt, R. J. (2005). Cultivating the moral character of learning and teaching: A neglected dimension of educational leadership. *School Leadership and Management, 25*(4), 399–411.

Stavy, R., and Tirosh, D. (2000). *How students (mis-)understand science and mathematics: Intuitive rules.* New York: Teachers College Press.

Stevens, R., Wineburg, S., Herrenkohl, L. R., and Bell, P. (2005). Comparative understanding of school subjects: Past, present, and future. *Review of Educational Research, 75*(2), 125–57.

Stiggins, Richard J. (2004). New assessment beliefs for a new school mission. *Phi Delta Kappan, 86*(1), 22–27.

Stipek, D. (2004). *Motivation to learn: From theory to practice.* 4th ed. Boston: Allyn & Bacon.

Tom, A. R. (1984). *Teaching as a moral craft.* New York: Longman.

Valli, L. (1990). Moral approaches to reflective practice. In R. T. Clift, W. R. Houston, and M. C. Pugach (Eds.), *Encouraging reflective practice in education: An analysis of issues and programs* (pp. 57–72). New York: Teachers College Press.

Valli, L., and Croninger, R. (2001). *High-quality teaching of foundational skills in mathematics and reading.* Washington, DC: National Science Foundation Interdisciplinary Educational Research Initiative.

Valli, L., Croninger, R., Alexander, P., Chambliss, M., Graeber, A., and Price, J. (2004, April). A study of high-quality teaching: Mathematics and reading. Symposium paper presented at the annual meeting of the American Educational Research Association. San Diego, CA.

Wiggins, G., and McTighe, J. (1998). *Understanding by design.* Alexandria, VA: Association for Supervision and Curriculum Development (ASCD).

Wilson, S. (1992). A case concerning content: Using case studies to teach about subject matter. In J. Shulman (Ed.), *Case methods in teacher education* (pp. 64–89). New York: Teachers College Press.

Woolfolk, A. (2001). *Educational psychology.* 8th ed. Boston: Allyn & Bacon.

Index

accelerated programs, 89, 90
advanced level classes, 101
affect, motivation and, 118–20
African Americans: students, 20, 20n4, 25, 39, 59, 70, 89, 101, 139; with subsidized lunch, 139; teachers, 20, 152
Alexander, P. A., 10, 11; on knowledge base, 117; on learning in situation or context, 121; on motivation and affect, 118; on strategic processing and executive functioning, 120
American Psychological Association (APA), 5
application, as central to understanding, 36–37
area: case, 71–76; case overview, 70; case setting, 69–70; concept of, 11–12; math case,

70; perimeter distinguished from, 69–76; questions, 76
Asian Americans: students, 20, 20n4, 29, 39, 59, 78, 89, 101, 139; with subsidized lunch, 139
attributes, 78, 86; for learning, 118; personal, 79, 82–84; of triangles, 79–80, 82. *See also* volume

Barnett-Clark, C., 8
behaviors, regulating, 120–21
Black, P., 147
Blankstein, A. M., 141
Borasi, R., 8

cases. *See* lesson cases; math cases
CAST. *See* Center for Applied Special Technology
CCSSO. *See* Council of Chief State School Officers

About the Contributors

Anna Graeber is associate professor emerita in the Department of Curriculum and Instruction at the University of Maryland, with her doctorate in mathematics education from Teachers College, Columbia University. For fifteen years she served in various mathematics curriculum and staff development positions at Research for Better Schools, a regional educational laboratory in Philadelphia. She is best known for her research on students' misconceptions in mathematics. Her research commonly uses structured, task-based interviews. She has served as an advisor on a number of dissertations employing qualitative research methods to document teachers' attempts to implement teaching in the spirit of the National Council of Teachers of Mathematics Professional Standards for Teaching Mathematics.

Linda Valli is the inaugural Jeffrey & David Mullan Professor of Teacher Education and Professional Development in the Department of Curriculum and Instruction at the University of Maryland. She has a Ph.D. from the Department of Education Policy Studies at the University of Wisconsin–Madison and served for ten years as the director of teacher education at the Catholic University of America, where she developed a research-based teacher education program and used cases in her own teaching. She now teaches graduate courses on research on teaching, professional development, and action research. Her publications focus on the context of teaching, learning to teach, culturally responsive pedagogy, and education policy. She has extensive experience in ethnographic and qualitative research methodology.

Kristie Jones Newton is an assistant professor in the Department of Curriculum, Instruction, and Technology in Education at Temple University whose research and teaching focuses on mathematics education. As a graduate student at the University of Maryland, she participated extensively in the development and conduct of the High-Quality Teaching study, contributed significantly to the selection and writing of the cases, piloted the cases in her undergraduate math methods class, and wrote commentaries for the *Facilitator's Guide*.

COMMENTATORS

Patricia Alexander is a distinguished scholar-teacher and professor in the Department of Human Development at the University of Maryland with research interests in the areas of expertise, domain learning, reading, and strategic processing.

Lisa Boté is a senior lecturer in the areas of teacher education and mathematics education in the Department of Curriculum and Instruction at the University of Maryland. Her research interests are in the areas of teacher learning and children's mathematical thinking.

Kathy Lynn Brake is a regional administrator who oversees school performance in a large public school district. Formerly, an elementary school principal for fifteen years, she has her doctorate in educational leadership from Bowie State University.

Daria Buese is an assistant professor at McDaniel College with interests in teaching expertise, teacher roles, and the moral dimensions of teaching.

Min-tun Chuang completed her doctoral studies in the area of second language education and culture at the University of Maryland with interests in biliteracy and language transfer. She is now an assistant professor in the Department of Foreign Languages at National Chiayi University in Taiwan.

Paula Maccini is an associate professor in the Department of Special Education at the University of Maryland with research interests in mathematics interventions and learning disabilities.

Rebecca Oxford is a distinguished scholar-teacher and professor emerita of second language education in the Department of Curriculum and Instruction at the University of Maryland with interests in motivation, strategies, socially mediated learning, and technology. Her current appointment is at the Air University where she is professor of language education and research in the Language Department of the U.S. Air Force Culture and Language Center.

Christine Peterson Tardif has been a fourth- through sixth-grade teacher in a large public school system for eight years. She has a bachelor's degree in animal science and a master's degree in education, both from the University of Maryland.